William Allen Butler

**Domesticus**

A tale of the Imperial city

William Allen Butler

**Domesticus**
*A tale of the Imperial city*

ISBN/EAN: 9783743382121

Manufactured in Europe, USA, Canada, Australia, Japa

Cover: Foto ©ninafisch / pixelio.de

Manufactured and distributed by brebook publishing software (www.brebook.com)

William Allen Butler

**Domesticus**

# A TALE OF THE IMPERIAL CITY

BY

## WILLIAM ALLEN BUTLER

NEW YORK
CHARLES SCRIBNER'S SONS
1886

# CONTENTS.

vi CONTENTS.

# CONTENTS.

## CHAPTER XX.

## CHAPTER XXI.

## CHAPTER XXII.

## CHAPTER XXIII.

## CHAPTER XXIV.

## CHAPTER XXV.

# DOMESTICUS.

## CHAPTER I.

### A NAMELESS PRINCESS.

IT was in the pre-Æsthetic period, before the age
of Greenbacks, in the Imperial City of the fair
realm of Magna Patria, that the Little Lady, whose
true story I am about to tell, first tripped forth on
the stage of social existence.   Her name was duly
heralded when she was married, and it will doubtless
be duly heralded when she dies, but in these pages
she must be as nameless as the old woman who lived
in a shoe, the young woman who walked in beauty
like the night, or any other of the celebrities of her
sex, ancient or modern, who have become known
to fame and dear to memory, but who have never
been formally introduced, by name, to any circle of
their admirers.

Nor is her personal appearance, at any point of
time, to be made the subject of minute description.
Neither her face nor her form can be outlined by
pen, pencil or sunbeam.   Imagination may picture
her the fairest of blondes, or the most brilliant of

brunettes, and invest her with all the charms that were ever inventoried, in fact or fiction. Possibly, all that fancy shall paint her will fall short of the original, around whose loveliness, as well as lineage, must be drawn a light veil of mystery and reserve. All else shall be plainly told.

To begin at the beginning, our Little Lady, like all heroines of history or romance, was born, once upon a time. If ever a lucky star twinkled over an infant's birth, it was over hers. If ever babe was born with a silver spoon in its mouth, she had a set of spoons before she had a set of teeth. All the good fairies who ever hovered over a sleeping mortal, newly laid in crib or cradle, made her pillow their daily and nightly rendezvous. If Luxury has a lap, she was dandled in it, and if Fortune carries a horn of plenty, it was emptied at her feet.

And so she grew, day and night, in sun and shower, through all happy seasons, the birds singing, the flowers blooming, the winds blowing, and the earth revolving, for her special satisfaction and delight, while Father Time counted out for her his reserve of golden moments, with reckless generosity, she spending them as freely, and making all faces brighter, and all hearts happier, wherever she came or went, as child, or maiden, until a merry clanging of bells rang in her wedding day.

For, of course, as the Little Lady had everything in plenty, lovers were not wanting, in due time. The good fairies supplied them in battalions. Never was fair damsel more beset by wooers and when at last, she was won and carried off in triumph by the favored suitor, it was over a legion of broken hearts.

The good fairies would have been strangely delinquent if they had permitted her to marry lower than a Prince; and, fortunately, a Prince it was who became her lawful, wedded husband. He was of the ancient and most honorable line of Merchant Princes, and his principality consisted of a vast stock of Dry Goods, the staple of his princely house, whose credit and renown all Magna Patria knew. He, too, had been under the fostering care of good fairies, and was supposed to possess all the various qualities out of which Deportment can create a model, and Business a success. He was very good-looking, very wise and very rich, and he had a modest palace of his own, on the Via Quinta, in the Imperial City. So, with no one to forbid the bans, this happy pair were wedded; Love and Friendship pelting them with flowers and pursuing them with rice, old slippers and horseshoes, and loading them with a weight and wealth of gifts which seemed to say, in the language of conveyancers—" Know all men by these presents, that the Merchant Prince, party of the first part, is held and firmly bound unto the Little Lady, party of the second part."

Now, the Little Lady, like all other favorites of good fairies, who have been waited upon from earliest infancy, and whose ideas of labor are bounded by the latest style of embroidery, had never bothered herself about anything under the sun. Having had a lovely time, all her life, before she wedded a Prince, she naturally counted on having a still lovelier time, now that she was a Princess. The first item of felicity on her programme was a honey-moon, to be spent in strange lands, far over sea, and this was happily accomplished, without a drawback, by the aid of a magical contrivance, at the Prince's command, known as an unlimited letter of credit, a wonderful talisman for all travellers, in Old Worlds or New.

But our Princess, being no bird of passage, and fondest of her own nest and nook, looked longingly and lovingly, from mountain top, and valley, and gay scenes in great cities, to the home of which she hoped to be the mistress and the household of which she expected to be the head. She would often sit, in silence and alone, in the twilight, turning, with two tiny fingers of her right hand, the plain golden circlet upon one tiny finger of her left hand, and think how precious a symbol it was of the sacred sphere in which she would be invested with a central and select sovereignty, and she was impatient to grasp the sceptre and begin her gentle reign. The happiest hour of her happy life seemed to her the one, in which, on the day of her safe return—the wide ocean and the broad continent left behind as pleasant memories—she sat, in the quiet evening, at her own table, in the palace of her Prince. He had prepared a rare surprise for her; and, by means of messages sent, by magical art, under sea, long in advance, had so arranged as to gather around his board, in her honor, the friends

she loved best, so that all things seemed ready to
her hand and heart, and she had only to seat herself
in the throne and be Queen. No wonder her eyes
sparkled with delight and her cheek glowed with
satisfaction. And when, late in the night, after the
last, lingering guest had departed, the Little Lady
walked up and down the stately rooms, pausing, now
and then, to survey herself in some resplendent
mirror, as if in reassurance of her own identity, or
to toy with some choice souvenir, or sit, for a
moment, in a gilded chair, her heart was well nigh
overflowing with happiness and hope. She could not
help dancing for very joy, and clapping her jeweled
hands she cried aloud—

"Now I am going to keep house!"

No sooner had the Little Lady uttered these words
than all the good fairies, who, as we have already seen,
had been busily engaged, ever since she was born,
in buttering her bread on both sides, gave a sudden
and unanimous, though inaudible, groan, shed a sim-
ultaneous, though invisible, tear, and waved a concerted and final, though imperceptible, farewell.

This was cruel, but it was inevitable; for it was
the immemorial law and custom of that region and
realm that whensoever any one, Princess or dame
of low degree, old or young, became a housekeeper,
all the good fairies who had been in active service
on her behalf, no matter for how long a time, or
with what good intentions and results, were immediately put upon the retired list, and a certain

malevolent spirit of the air and minister of chaos
superseded them, and took entire charge and command, in their place and stead. Now this malignant
genius was named DOMESTICUS.

And it was on this wise with Domesticus. When
any lady of the land, little or large, went to housekeeping, he must be summoned. He was sure to
respond to the call, for this was his designated and
predestined task and duty; and, as he loved mischief
more than he hated work, he was always at hand,
and would appear on command, by word of mouth,
or on the customary ringing of a bell. But, like
Proteus of old, from whom, it may be, he had
descended, he had a million different shapes, and
there was no one so wise as to know, beforehand,
under what aspect he would come, of what race, or
age, or sex, or presence, or what name he would
use, for he could transform himself, at will, and was
a wonderfully ingenious and inventive spirit, and
incomprehensible withal.

The Little Lady had often heard about Domesticus and his doings, but she had never feared him,
partly because courage, and not fear, was natural to
her, partly because she had never bestowed much
thought upon him, but chiefly because she was
always so inclined to think well of every one and
everything that she had brought herself to entertain
a good opinion even of this wicked sprite. She had
been told many things concerning him, and always
to his disadvantage, by her relatives, lineal and
collateral. She knew he had a bad name, but, to

tell the truth, that bad name of his had rather attracted her sympathies toward Domesticus. She was so full of all human pity and tenderness that her heart had, somehow, gone out to him, in the vague hope that whenever, in her future happy life, she should come into closer contact with him, she might be able to do something to reclaim him and make him as good and lovely as she was herself, and as she wanted all the world to be. If she should ever have a palace of her own, she wanted it to be a bower of bliss, wherein even Domesticus himself would be subdued to the spirit of the place, and become docile and dutiful, out of sheer sympathy. If he should come to her in manly form, he would thus, although a servitor, be invested with a knightly sense of loyalty and chivalry ; and if he should be represented by one of her own sex, she would grow to be as graceful and neat handed as Hebe. All this, and more, in a gush of girlish feeling, she had once confided to a grim-visaged aunt, at whose palace she chanced to be a guest, and who, being of mature age, and, at the time, under a special infliction and visitation of Domesticus, tartly told her that she was a green girl and knew no more about this arch enemy than the babe unborn.

But now she has ceased to be a green girl, and she is in her own house and home, with the will and the way to work out to their fulfillment all these bright and beneficent designs and, on the morrow, her gentle hand shall be laid on the monster's neck and leviathan shall be tamed.

# CHAPTER II.

THE sun rose, on the following morning, in a
cloudless sky, over the Imperial City. Its
shrines and temples, its Forum and its many palaces, threw back, from pediment and tower and
clustered roofs, the bright early beams, as they fell
upon the great wedge-shaped city, lying between
two noble rivers whose confluence formed a spa-
cious harbor where the ships of many nations came
and went; for the Imperial citizens were traders
with all the world. And yet, strange to say, in
their perverseness, while they scooped out and
fashioned deep basins and slips on the sides of both
rivers, wherein the myriad vessels of all countries
could float and have safe shelter and mooring, they
dumped the soil and dredgings from these same
basins and slips into the waters of the narrow and
sinuous channels, leading from the harbor to the
deep sea, so as to block and hinder the access and
egress of the very commerce for which they provided at such pains. This was of a piece with all
their municipal methods, and may serve to show
what little progress they had made in the great
science of local government, which, nearer home,

8

we have brought to such rare perfection. But, aside from a continuing and chronic mal-adminis- tration, it was a fair and prosperous metropolis, wherein the ineradicable civic indifference to the pub- lic weal was counterpoised by a ceaseless eagerness and skill in private enterprise; and so it grew in wealth and power, with steady growth. Nor was there, in the wide world, a city where hands and hearts were more readily opened to the cry of want or suffering, or quicker to aid in all good works for human kind.

The palace of our Prince was within the selected limits set apart, by common consent of the citizens, to patrician dwellings, and consecrated to an all- powerful divinity, Societas by name, whose votaries were numerous, and whose priestesses were versed in many mysteries and held sway over all who dwelt or came within the charmed circle of their influence. Like all the houses of its class, in the pre-Æsthetic period of Magna Patria, it was a mar- vel of exterior clumsiness and of interior unfitness. Many sestertia of the lawful money of the realm had gone from the Prince's purse into bulky, out- side stone work, hideous to the eye, and into mon- strous products of the deforming arts of plasterers, upholsterers, and decorators, equally abhorrent, within doors, and many more into a net-work of leaden conduits by which, under false pretences of cleanliness and comfort, poisoned air and death- dealing gases were made to permeate every nook and corner of the mansion.

But, according to their light, and after their blundering fashion, the patricians of the Imperial City made for themselves elegant and luxurious habitations, whose appliances for warmth, and light, and convenience, in many ways, were far superior to those existing, at the time, in the best dwelling-houses of Mater Patria, the main source from which the Imperial citizens derived their ideas of home with all its traditional environment of good things.

To the Little Lady, the palace was a supreme satisfaction and, aided by the sense of security and rest with which it seemed to be pervaded on the night of her arrival, her slumbers were undisturbed and long protracted. The Prince was early astir and abroad, leaving the palace without waiting for his morning meal, which he expected to take in that quarter of the Imperial City in which his principality lay. The Princess, considerately left to her repose, did not rise until the day was well advanced and the bustle on the broad Avenue, on which she looked out from her windows, seemed to rebuke her for having slept so long. Her happy thoughts immediately took up again the golden thread they had dropped as she had fallen asleep. She was now, more than ever, the mistress of the mansion and of the model home to be created within its walls. She knew that the service of the previous evening had been improvised for the occasion, according to the directions of the Prince, who, in his wisdom, had confided the arrangements to a junior of his house, versed in the arts and mysteries

of Dry Goods, and specially familiar, as one of the
ancient and worshipful guild of Salesmen, with all
manner of festive rites. He had easily contrived
the entertainment and loaded the Prince's board
with good cheer, providing, among other choice
exotics, the skilled attendants who vanished when
their work was done, leaving the palace, swept
from the crumbs of the supper and garnished with
the flowers of the table, ready for the coming of
Domesticus.

The fore-thought of the Prince had looked beyond
the evening repast and made some provision for the
immediate wants of his household. Through the
same friendly intervention, Domesticus had been
summoned, and the Princess was shown a trig and
twinkling-eyed damsel, flitting about the palace, in
the guise of a housemaid who, as it seemed to her,
might be the ideal Hebe of her fancy, and she was
also told that there was a perfect Treasure below
stairs. To this extent had the prudent Prince
undertaken to settle the preliminaries of what he
hoped might be a lasting peace with Domesticus,
little knowing the crafty adversary with whom he
had to deal.

The Princess, after getting wide awake and nearly
dressed, was somewhat puzzled to conjecture what
had become of the neat-handed Hebe on this bright
morning, and why she was not at her door, betimes,
with proffers of aid and service meet for the toilette
of a lady of her high degree. But she came not,
nor was the sound of dust pan, hand brush or

broom to be heard in the halls or on the staircase, nor was she to be seen, when the Little Lady, inquisitively and somewhat furtively, took an observation with her door ajar. Then she bethought her that Hebe was doubtless busied in arranging a dainty repast for her mistress—a satisfactory solution, not that the Little Lady, any more than any other well-conditioned Princess, cared, in the least, what she had to eat or drink in the morning, or at noon, or night, but because, in her new relation to it, as the head of the house, breakfast began to appear to her in the light of an Institution. It would be necessarily incomplete on this first morning, as the Prince was absent, and the great chest of silver had, ever since the wedding day, lain undisturbed in the vaults of Aurum & Argentum, the great conjurers who could transmute anybody's and everybody's gold and silver into tea sets, dinner sets, jewelry and all the other necessaries of life, and then keep them safe and sound, at moderate rates of storage. Only a special and unique service of small, antique silver, a few rare and costly pieces, had the Prince brought home with him from the Old World; these had been exhibited and admired during the evening, and left in the unlocked drawer of the onyx-topped buffet, the Princess taking no thought of the fact that, from time immemorial, it had been the invariable custom and duty of every good housekeeper to cradle such treasures in a basket, and take them as nearly to bed with her as circumstances would permit.

When the Princess had ended her toilette, and

taken a final look at herself in the glass, she went
down stairs. The house was dark, in spite of the
brilliancy of the outer day, and an ominous chill
struck through her as she entered the room she had
last quitted the night before, and found it still
unopened. No ray of enlivening sunshine greeted
her at the threshold of the banqueting hall, but only
light enough to disclose, at a glance, that no dainty
repast, nor any visible sign of its preparation, was
in view. The room was still, and cold, and vacant,
but the quick eye of the Princess, taking in everything on the instant, perceived that the upper
drawer of the buffet in which had been deposited,
over night, the Prince's precious pieces of small
silver, was open. A swift, prophetic pang shot
through her soul; she rushed to the drawer and
the truth flashed upon her. Hebe, the neat handed
but light fingered, had fled, and, with her, all the
small silver, every ounce, every pennyweight, every
grain.

This was the first sword thrust of Domesticus.
If it did not pierce the Little Lady's heart, it was
only because he never despatched his victims at
once, but loved to keep them at his cruel mercy.
The Princess did not sink, nor scream, nor swoon.
She simply stood aghast. But, even in her surprise
and horror, she cast no railing accusation against
Domesticus, or his emissary, the fugitive Hebe;
but only heaped reproach upon her own sweet self,
putting no blame on the Prince, or on the junior
prince, who had brought this serpent into her Eden.

"It is all my fault, my fault," she said, "I ought to have taken it up stairs when I went to bed."

Then, as the question came home to her, "What am I to do?" her thought reverted to the Treasure below as her sole immediate refuge and succor. The bell was close at hand, and she rang it with a quick, convulsive jerk, which set in motion a distant, half smothered, discordant tingle, which seemed like the suppressed, mocking laughter of some concealed demon. She well knew that the bell was the summons of Domesticus, but if he were represented, in those subterranean precincts of the palace, by a Treasure, there was nothing to dread, and if the Treasure would not come to the Princess, the Princess must go to the Treasure. And this, after long, unanswered ringings of the bell, she determined to do, much wondering what might next befall her in her new domain.

She descended to the lower floor, and as the door which admitted her into this unexplored territory closed behind her, found herself in deeper darkness than before. A glimmer of light showed what she divined must be the penetralia of the Treasure, because in one corner she descried the outline of the tall cylindrical boiler, lifted, like a huge foreboding finger, to warn her off. But she took no heed and pressed on, not looking downward, and so, not seeing the obstruction which blocked her way, a mass of matter in human shape, against which she stumbled and across which she fell, her fair forehead striking the hard floor, on

which she lay stunned and unconscious. The Little
Lady had tumbled over the Treasure; the unpleasant
tale of whose temptation and fall an empty flagon, in
close proximity to her prostrate form, too plainly told.

Of the subsequent events of that eventful morning,
the Little Lady could never give a satisfactory explanation to herself, or to any one else. She has a
vague recollection of a return to consciousness, and
of seeing, in shadowy outline, the uniformed and
helmeted figure of a Curator of the public peace,
who, having kept special watch and ward over the
palace, during the absence of the Prince, was surprised, on the morning after his return, to find the
iron door, which led into its lower regions, wide
open, as it had been swung back by the departing
Hebe, the order of whose going had not stood upon
leaving closed doors behind her. Accordingly, in
the due discharge of his duty, the Curator entered,
to survey the premises, at the opportune moment of
the catastrophe I have just described. Deserted as
she was by all the good fairies, and sore beset as
she was by Domesticus, it seemed a wonderful piece
of good fortune that such aid and comfort should
have come to the Little Lady in her extremity, but
she is firmly persuaded that this was the manner of
her deliverance, and she never looked, thereafter, at
one of the big-buttoned corps to which her deliverer
belonged, without a thrill of gratitude. It was he
who conveyed the Princess, up the stairs, to the
nearest lounge, and who conveyed the Treasure,
down the street, to the nearest lock-up.

A bevy of the Little Lady's friends of her own sex and age happened to come tripping along, shortly afterwards, to tender their congratulations on her safe return and to inspect her new home, and although their congratulations were congealed into condolence, they were very helpful to her in her sore distress. They sat about her, bathing her bruised brow, administering all the restoratives within reach, and, like the chorus of a Greek play, making the air resound with alternate bursts of sympathy for the Little Lady and maledictions against Domesticus. Each one had her special recital of his misdeeds, recent and remote, a dark catalogue of unwritten and unpunishable crimes, against which there was no relief and no redress, and which were filling the bosoms of families with gloom and despair. So the lovely choristers surrounded the Princess, thrusting out their tiny, high-heeled boots, waving their snow-white, bangled arms, shaking their jeweled fists, and almost shrieking, as they recounted these unnumbered woes.

The fair visitants did not confine themselves to the chorus; they gave all heed to ministering to the wants of the victim of Domesticus, and to that end, went through all the doors, drawers and cupboards, up stairs and down stairs, as if they had been armed with search-warrants, and foraged throughout the premises for whatever might be serviceable in the emergency. Nothing came of it all, except a single cup of tea, which they served with a vast amount of laughing, and chattering, and merriment, at finding

themselves in a palace actually, for the time being,
deserted by Domesticus. It was, in reality, a pillaged outpost, which had been stormed, and sacked,
and then left behind by the invader, but to the
young ladies, it seemed only like a great house
having a holiday, and enjoying it in silence. So
they rummaged about, without let or hindrance. If
there had been a skeleton in any closet, it would
have been brought to light, but the closets were
bare, as the Little Lady's boxes had not been
unpacked, and as she ruefully said, she had nothing
to show her friends except her own damaged face.

2

# CHAPTER III.

## A NEW DEPARTURE.

MEANWHILE, not Rumor with her hundred tongues, but the faithful Curator with his single brogue, had brought to the Prince the tidings of the disaster. He lost no time in setting in motion so much of the detective enginery of the law as lay within his reach, for the pursuit and apprehension of the fugitive and spoliating Hebe; and then hurried homeward, with the help of such substitutes for seven-league boots as the prosaic character of the times on which he had fallen would permit. On his way, he bethought him that the Princess, in her helpless condition, would be wholly without the means of carrying on the affairs of the household, and the prospect of possible starvation not being a pleasant one, he determined to go, at once, to a neighboring and friendly sorcerer, supposed to be on the most familiar terms with Domesticus, as one of a guild by whose agency, to a large extent, his countless emissaries were quartered on the inhabitants of the Imperial City.

This sorcerer, in common with all of his fraternity who possessed and plied the same magical arts,

18

was able to command, at will, the presence of the varied shapes in which Domesticus appeared for every variety of service. Like the slaves of the lamp in the Arabian Nights, they came, when summoned, at the bidding of their superiors, whose dens were easy of access, so that any and all householders, driven to seek the aid of Domesticus, were free to come and try their fortune with the help of the sorcerer, who by his art could call these visible spirits from contiguous deeps, not vast, but, usually, quite circumscribed, redolent with divers odors, and confused with the noise of many tongues.

These sorcerers, as a spell to conjure with, contrived to press into their service that honest polysyllabic word "Intelligentia"; they painted it, in large characters, over all their lintels as if they were, in some sort, the specially accredited dispensers and custodians of intelligence, whereas the commodities in which they dealt were often at the farthest remove from any such faculty, but this was only another of the many strange devices of Domesticus. So our Prince thought himself well served, when after divers incantations, the sorcerer caused a succession of shapes to pass before him, from which he made careful selection, and was assured that they would re-appear at his summons, within his palace, and do his bidding and that of the Princess, in all things, and strange to say, the Prince, with all his wisdom, went his way firmly believing these promises would be fulfilled ; such was the glamour which Domesticus and his cunning allies, the sorcerers, could cast over the strongest and clearest minds.

But when the Prince came to his Lady's chamber, and told her what he had done for her solace and comfort, she refused to be comforted. Domesticus had given her what he had given thousands of her patient, suffering sex afore-time, a headache, of his own peculiar and malevolent invention, which made its victims turn a deaf ear and a sightless eye to every word or sign of consolation. So the Prince was forced to sit solitary at his board, while the Princess bemoaned her fate, above stairs, and Domesticus gloated, in secret, over the misery he had wrought in the first calamity this loving pair had encountered.

The destructive work of this first day, complete as it may seem, was only a harsh prelude and discordant overture to what Domesticus had in store for the Little Lady. He well knew she was brave of heart and stout of will, and not to be crushed at a blow, and he kept in reserve many a heated plowshare, over which he meant her path should lie. And brave of heart and stout of will she was, emerging from this first, fiery ordeal somewhat crest-fallen and chagrined, but not bating hope or courage, and with faith soon re-established in her future.

Nor was she one whit disheartened by the flurry and storm which followed the Prince's venture with the sorcerer, the outcome of which was nothing but dire failure. The Prince soon came to see that with all his good intention and amiable action, excused, if not justified, by the emergency of the case, he had really been playing into the hands of Domesticus, who, being himself an arch disorgan- izer, was never so well pleased as when the house- hold order was subverted by such irregular pro- ceedings as this one on the part of the Prince. He had, in his supposed wisdom, but real folly, rushed in where even the angels of well conducted homes feared to tread. He had violated the cardinal law by which the peace of familics subsists. He had rashly usurped a function which belonged exclu- sively to the Princess. Not that she, sweet soul, complained, but that Domesticus maliciously made use of this infraction as a weapon of torture, and instructed the new comers that as they had enlisted at the call of the Prince they owed no allegiance or duty to the Princess, and accordingly, so soon as she assumed command, they were in open revolt. The poor Prince's efforts to compel subordination were wholly ineffectual, and his carefully selected and picked corps deserted and decamped.

The reins once more in her own hands, as she fondly hoped, the Princess determined to make a bold push to assert herself and her supremacy. Then it was that in her own right, and in her own behalf, she consulted the sorcerers and found, to her dismay, that while they were on the alert to serve her, the spirits whom they called came not only in questionable but most questioning shapes. She, who came to examine, and scrutinize, and select, suddenly, by some strange witchery and transformation, was turned into an object of suspicion, to be herself cross-examined, catechised, weighed in balances, and, too often, found wanting. How many were there in family? Was there a baby? Did they eat by courses? How early did they get up? How late did they go to bed? Would there be somebody else to do everybody's work? She was made to feel like a culprit before a committing magistrate, without a culprit's privilege of waiving an examination, or declining to criminate herself, and she was glad to escape from the grasp of her inquisitors, with a mingled sense of humiliation and defeat.

Then it was that her wants were, according to the custom of the place, heralded on all the columns, set up for this purpose, in the Imperial City. Then it was she discovered that Domesticus had so sapped and subverted the foundations of morality, that mankind in general, and womankind in particular, claimed to be absolved from every obligation of truth or veracity in certifying as to his representatives. He seemed to have granted a kind of dispensation in the use of the vernacular, whereby such old time terms as "sobriety," "honesty," "industry," "fidelity," and the like, were no longer real names for real qualities, but were reduced to the level of mere trademarks, labels, and brands, for the wares of Domesticus, who so juggled and contrived with these and other devices, as to delude a confiding public into the notion that all the virtues could be hired at a fixed rate per month—a draft on popular credulity which would have been dishonored at sight in any other sphere of sublunary affairs.

Then, moreover, it was that the Little Lady kept on courageously ringing her bell, and Domesticus kept making his appearance, in all the wonderful, inexhaustible variety of his forms. Sometimes he would come in what seemed to be personified slowness, and then everything was irretrievably behind time, whereat the Prince was greatly exercised, because Punctuality was a prime virtue of Dry Goods, and Domesticus, with his ally Procrastination, the thief of Time, made a pair better fitted for a Penitentiary than a Palace. Then he would appear in a tearing, slashing shape, so that the Prince and Princess were whirled along the courses of a meal, as though they were eating for a wager depending on the speed of the performance. The next incumbent would be of a pattern so small that the evening lamps could not be lighted without the aid of chairs, or the tall windows locked without step-ladders; to be replaced, anon, by some stalwart figure, marching and countermarching as if trained in the ranks of Penthesile, Queen of the Amazons. One day, it would be stupidity, in densest form, under whose confusing misdirection, Princes, and Princesses, and other notables, would be left standing in the vestibule, while vagrants, in disguise, were ceremoniously ushered into the inner precincts, whence they could slyly retire with any chance souvenir available to their thievish touch. The next incumbent would possess a rarely endowed intelligence, coupled, perhaps, with an undiscovered and undiscoverable mystery, given to the rehearsing of dramatic or lyric fragments in the stilly night, in close proximity to speaking tubes or furnace flues, quite too high strung and high toned for daily service.  But how often did Domesticus delight in tormenting and tantalizing the Little Lady with some well seeming maiden form, fair to see, full of sweetest promise, and shortest lived performance, making the household work, for the time, a delightsome thing and a forecast of permanent peace, but, presently, loving the youthful green-grocer, or the stalwart butcher, not wisely but too well, and thereupon becoming as limp as one of her own dish-cloths, and losing all working or waking sense in Love's young dream. For such an one the daily round of duty would soon give way to picnics, predestined invariably to take place in bedraggling thunder-squalls, or to midnight entertainments, requiring a fortnight to prepare for them, and three weeks to recover from them all, ending, too often, in the final exchange of the certain and safe shelter and comfort of a well-ordered home for a blank in the lottery of a chance marriage.

Yes, Domesticus was not only, as I have already said, like Proteus with his myriad shapes; he was like Argus with his hundred eyes, or Briareus with his hundred hands, or the Hydra with his many heads.  In fact, he was worse than these old offenders, because, while they, severally and respectively,

belonged to some specific nation or place, and had
a well defined pedigree of their own, Domesticus
could assume any nationality at pleasure, and change,
as he saw fit, his name, his country, or his skin, as
well as his spots, which he was always changing,
for he no sooner got comfortably into one than he
was uncomfortably on the outlook for another.

He was an arch cosmopolitan. His drag net was
thrown over every nook and corner of the globe; it
seemed to the Princess as if her premises were a
sort of rendezvous for all its races. Now, it was
Domesticus Anglicanus, who had stood, in state,
behind Dukes and Earls, and had come, at last, to
assert his supremacy as a sovereign, among his
fellow sovereigns of Magna Patria. Now, it was
Domesticus Gallicus, whose *cordon-bleu* was the
unfailing symbol of revolution and anarchy, below
stairs. Then, it was Domesticus Scotus, as obsti-
nately resolute to upset all pre-existing order at a
single blow, as was Jenny Geddes to topple over the
Papacy with a toss of her wooden stool. Again, it
was Domesticus Germanicus, whose coming and
going were like blasts from the forests of Norse-
land, and the hidden things of whose culinary compounds no one could discover or digest. But
chiefly, and at all times, it was Domesticus Hibernicus, the most constant and the most centrifugal of
all the forces that Labor ever contrived for the service
and discipline of mankind, and let loose upon un-
suspecting householders, with its conservation of
destructive energy; its readiness to make or mar;

its possibilities of chance success and its illimitable incapacity, alike unendurable and indispensable; the two-edged, unsheathed sword of the adversary, always sharpened with ready wit and pointed for instant action, and poised for cut or thrust—at once a social defence and a social terror.

What the Little Lady did, and what she suffered during this period of her warfare with Domesticus, cannot be recounted in detail. What wars of contending races were waged with her cutlery, and what fires of persecution were kindled with her coal, it would take too long to tell. The wrath roused into action between the contending votaries of rival shrines and opposing altars was unextinguishable, and the Little Lady came, at last, to think that Domesticus could make an *auto da fé* or a love feast minister equally to his malignant purposes, and that he could transform Religion herself into a Fury. Heretics who abjured the Pontifex Maximus and denounced him and his works were driven out, at the point of the boning knife and the larding pin, while they, in turn, pommelled his devout adherents with gridiron and saucepan, until the Little Lady in despair, like Gallio, drove the contending zealots from her jurisdiction, and was sorely tempted to supplement her next declaration of wants with the startling suffix—" Atheists preferred ! "

Thus everything went wrong; her pillow was wet with many tears during the long vigils of the night, and her heart strings were stretched, by day, to their utmost tension. But they never broke. Sometimes, there were gleams of hope and a vista of prospective peace, but only at brief intervals and for short periods of time. Of course, her one great, animating idea was to please the Prince, who was nothing if not hospitable, and who loved to see the Princess in her grace and beauty, presiding over a well-spread board, surrounded by congenial spirits. With all his wisdom, he could never be quite brought to comprehend why anything and everything which pleased his appetite, and ministered to his satisfaction, in other places or palaces, could not be made immediately, and permanently, available under his own roof. This was one of the many deep and subtile contrivances of Domesticus. Nothing was more to his depraved taste than to plant the germs of dissatisfaction in the sacred soil of home, by pointing sharp contrasts between its necessary limitations and the large possibilities beyond it. The Prince, for whose daily noontide refreshment, or occasional evening social delectation, when elsewhere than in his palace, there was the ready service of hands skilled to minister to every variety of taste, and proficient in the arts they exercised, was too apt to fancy that a like degree of perfection was an easy thing to attain within his own domicile.

Or, perchance, he would sit, a serenely satisfied, but wholly irresponsible guest, at some symposium, contrived at special pains and outlay, and bring home minute reminiscences of its completeness and perfection, every one of which would send a pang through the bosom of the Princess. She strove and struggled and endured; she braced herself for every fresh encounter with Domesticus; she sat through tedious hours of entertainment, with the heroism, if not the serenity, of a martyr at the stake, silent and uncomplaining, dreading disaster with every dish, from the opening demi-valve to the closing demi-tasse; apprehensive, from the moment she missed the salt in the soup to the moment when she found it in the ice cream; conscious of every blunder; self-condemning at every slip; and only too glad to fly, at the earliest moment of escape, from what seemed a throne of queenly state, but was, in reality, a rack of torture.

# CHAPTER IV.

EVERY intelligent reader who has followed thus far, in these pages, the fortunes and misfortunes of the Little Lady, will understand that she was by no means solitary and alone in her state of suffering. Of this she herself was well aware, but so staunch was her courage and so strong her will, that for a long time, she carried on the unequal warfare, single handed, seeking no succor, but like Ajax, in his long, midnight combat, only praying for light, that she might not be left wholly at the mercy of her foe, who was at home in the darkness and loved it better than the light.

After a series of successive defeats, culminating in her apparent total discomfiture, as she sat one day, curled up, as she was wont to describe her position, in a favorite and capacious easy chair in her own quiet solarium, or sunny boudoir, to which she often resorted for meditation and repose, and after donning her invisible thinking cap, and revolving in her mind the many instances of her weakness and want of ability to cope with her wily enemy, she came to feel the absolute need of some friendly help and counsel. It was sad to be forced to the conclusion that neither love nor money would avail to win over this inveterate foe, or to counteract his evil ways. Of love, she had by nature an inexhaustible supply, and of money, the Prince was lavish, and what could not these potent forces effect ? What, indeed, except the conquest of Domesticus ? Thus musing, she formed a sudden resolve which was promptly executed. A few moments of preparation sufficed, and with the lightest of footsteps, if not with the lightest of hearts, she made her way to a neighboring palace, where dwelt an ancient and venerable housekeeper whose sage counsel she proposed to seek.

The name of this wisest of women was the Princess Pugnax. She was a veteran dowager of vast experience, within doors and without. She had a reputation among housewives which could not be excelled, if indeed it could be equalled. Her mahogany, her oil cloths, her brasses, her silver, her linen, were the envy of her contemporaries. They were quoted in social circles, as government bonds are quoted at the Stock Exchange and in Bank parlors. You could eat off her floors; the heaviest finger could be drawn over the polished tops of her mantels or tables without detecting a particle of dust; her pantries and presses could be opened at any hour of the day or· night, without revealing a sign of disorder; her furniture looked as if it were on a perpetual dress-parade. It was generally believed that she had beaten Domesticus on his own ground. The current and accepted

report was that she had established a Reign of Terror
in her precincts, and set up a permanent guillotine,
as the only effectual method of dealing with
Domesticus and his representatives, and that she
had achieved a signal success. It was said that
decapitations were as common with her as dinners.
Sometimes, the whole force would be dealt with
summarily, by a preconcerted *coup d'état*, and
there would be a head in the kitchen sink ; another
in the butler's tray ; a third in the laundry tubs ; a
fourth in the sewing basket ; a fifth in the housemaid's dustpan, and so on, according to the various
appliances in use in the mansions of the Imperial
City, of which those I have specified are the equiv-
alents in our own metropolis. Domesticus, with
his ready resources and magic art, could, it is true,
always contrive to rescue his votaries, however
mangled, as easily as Minerva protected her *proté-
gés* in the Homeric wars, spiriting them away, putting the missing heads on the right shoulders, or
supplying new ones, and forming out of these
restored victims a kind of old guard for his more
perilous enterprises. Then he would invade the
Pugnax territory with fresh levies, who would, in
turn, be routed and destroyed by the relentless
Princess, whose reputation rose with each successive slaughter, until she ranked as a Field-Mar-
shal or Generalissimo among surrounding Princesses. But as the reserves and munitions of war
of Domesticus were inexhaustible, the faster the
gaps in his ranks were made, the faster they were

filled, and as it was in his savage nature to feel a kind of grim satisfaction in the misery even of his own followers, he took a double delight in the heavy load he laid on the Princess, and the burdens she imposed on them. In truth, he was well satisfied to let her have an apparent supremacy, well knowing it was only titular, and that she was, really, as much in vassalage to him as was Herod the Great to the Roman Cæsar. So, if ever there was a victrix victim it was the Princess Pugnax. Her reputation had to be maintained, and in order to keep her record at its high standard, her whole life became a succession of campaigns and dearly bought victories, the price of a seeming triumph over the wily Domesticus and his hobgoblin legions. Meanwhile, she openly and persistently defied him and maintained a brave show of independence, and due respect was paid her accordingly.

In the case of the Little Lady, this respect amounted almost to awe, and she thought herself very bold to ask help, in her sore straits, from this lofty dame. She approached her as an oracle and divulged the story of her griefs, in an ascending scale of intensity which reached its climax with the despairing cry—"What am I to do with Domesticus?"

The chief characteristic of the Princess Pugnax was rigidity. Her form was rigid, her features were rigid, her dress was rigid. Nature and Time had kept her so submerged in the indurating waters of

strife that she seemed to have suffered a gradual
process of petrifaction. Her glance was stony, her
voice was hard, and her fingers closed on the Little
Lady's hand, like the claw of an extinct animal.
There was no spot on her hardened nature to soften
at the tears, or melt at the sorrows, of her weaker
sister. She heard her confession, and passed sen-
tence upon her, without delay or preface, as upon a
self-condemned criminal. It was all the Little
Lady's own wilful fault. It was all for the want of
a little order, a little forethought, and a little firm-
ness. The strong hand and the tight rein had been
lacking. Had she rung up Domesticus in the
morning? Had she seen that every living human
being, in the house, was in bed, before she closed her
own eyes for the night? Had she kept everything
under lock and key? Had she proper weights and
measures? Had she given out the things herself?

The Little Lady was painfully conscious that she
had given out, in a very different sense from that
which the dowager intended, but she admitted that
she had been derelict at all points, whereupon she
was given to understand that she was a doomed
woman. Domesticus was an enemy, against whom
not to take the initiative was to be lost in advance.
In the war with him there was no quarter and no
discharge. His emissaries were outlaws, for whom
there should be no amnesty; sleepless vigilance,
incessant marches, counter-marches, bivouacs, sur-
prises, captures and massacres must be the order of
the day and of the night. It was a life-long cru-

3

sade, with no summer quarters, no winter quarters, no truces, not even a parley between pickets. The Little Lady sat aghast at the deliverances of this scarred veteran as she showed how fields in this way might be won in the warfare with Domesticus, and how, by any other art or articles of war, they were sure to be lost. Domesticus, she said, was the arch enemy of all order. His hand was against everything, from a pewter cup to the stars in their courses. The great desire of his wicked heart was the reign of universal breakage, and confusion, and ruin; and unless vows were made on all the household altars of the land that he himself should be bound, hand and foot, and brought into due subjection, chaos would come again.

"But is the fault all on the side of Domesticus?" said the Little Lady.

"Certainly it is. Whose fault can it be but his? It is the total, universal depravity of his nature."

"But may not moral suasion have some effect?"

"Moral fiddlesticks! Have you never heard the story of Gehazi? He is a good specimen of the whole race. If his master could not keep him from going to the bad, what can a poor housewife do, who cannot work miracles and cure lepers?"

"And you really think there is no room or hope for improvement?" said the Little Lady, sadly and softly.

"Not the least; things will wax worse and worse. The great point with Domesticus is to get the most wages for the least labor; what he wants is to play, instead of working, to rule instead of serving, to get all the ignorant, inefficient housekeepers under his thumb, and to fasten on them the curse of being made the servants of servants."

Just at this point there was a sound as of the distant crash of falling china, and the Princess Pugnax started, and sprang to her feet, with a jarring movement, as if a whole system of unoiled machinery had suddenly been set in motion by some irresistible, unseen force.

" I gave her warning last night, for being in the house five minutes late and this is her revenge. Excuse me a moment, my dear."

" I must go now; thank you, very, very much, for your good advice," said the Little Lady, rising and taking leave, only too glad to cut short her visit, under cover of the catastrophe which, she felt sure, was impending in the Pugnax palace.

# CHAPTER V.

## WEIGHTS AND MEASURES.

SHE came out, into the sunshine of the street, as
from a prison house of despair. She seemed to
herself like an escaped convict, liable at any instant
to re-arrest. She had gone for comfort, and had
received condemnation. She had asked for bread,
and had been given a stone. Happily, she was of a
temperament buoyant enough to make the best of
everything, and so to find sermons, with practical
applications, even in the stones which the Princess
Pugnax had thrown at her. She would put into
immediate practice a part of the Pugnax system.
She would provide a bell for rousing the sound
sleepers on her top story, and she would ring it
herself, gently, but firmly. She would have patent
scales and a steelyard, and some standard weights
and measures, but these could be adjusted and employed with a gracious touch as well as with the
cruel hand of an executioner. She would give out
all the things herself, but it should be done with a
smile and not a frown. It was not in her nature to
substitute law, all at once, for love. Her whole
being revolted against the cold, harsh doctrine of
the stony-visaged dame, and yet, if order, and firm-

ness, and a tight rein, were the prime conditions of success, a little severity in appearance, which could always be tempered by underlying tenderness, might be desirable, if not indispensable.

Accordingly, the next break of dawn inaugurated the new campaign. The Prince was startled from his morning nap by a harsh jingle, such as had never before disturbed his repose, and awoke to descry the Princess tugging at a stout silken rope, pendent on the wall, within easy reach of her pillow. Her hair was dishevelled, and her eyes were somewhat wild, for she had lain awake half the night in order to be ready to ring the bell at the proper and appointed moment, but there was a fixed purpose in every pull of the cord, and even in the pause which followed its vibrations.

"What are you about?" asked the Prince.

The Princess briefly explained that this was the beginning of new and better things; that the bell which startled him, because it was an unusual sound, was one to which he would soon become accustomed; that it was to ring out all laziness and sleepiness from the household, and ring in a time of better breakfasts, and general domestic bliss.

The Prince did not think she could keep it up.

She was determined to keep it up if it kept her up all night.

"Suppose you should be ill?"

She would have to be very ill, yes at death's door, before she would be unable to reach the bell cord; besides she was not ill, but unusually well, and hoped to keep so.

" Suppose they won't get up? "

" Then they will all have to go."

"Suppose there should be guests in the palace and they should be waked out of their best sleep, at such an unseasonable hour, what would they think ? "

" They would think they were in a place where order reigned, which is heaven's first law, and ought therefore to be enforced as early in the morning as possible. Besides, have you not always insisted that guests must take the risk of whatever goes on in the house they visit? "

" Ordinary risks, yes, but this is something extra-ordinary," said the Prince.

" What is there extraordinary about it? The Princess Pugnax has done it for years and years, and you ought to be glad and thankful if I can do as well as she does."

"I don't believe it will last," said the Prince, sighing over his lost nap.

" That is the way you always discourage me," said the Princess, and she repressed some unavailing tears, while the stony-hearted Prince closed his eyes and started to count the odd numbers, from one to five thousand, in the hope of thereby reinstating himself in the slumber from which he had been so rudely roused.

Betimes, on the same day, everything eatable and drinkable, every bar and cake of soap, every box of matches, every paper of starch, every grain of salt, was secured behind locked doors, and the process of giving out by weight and measure was begun, with a degree of solemnity which was meant to be most impressive, but which, in the irreverent eyes of Domesticus, was so supremely comical that if he had had any visible sides he would have split them with laughter.

When the Prince came home to dinner, he found the Little Lady wearing a strangely defiant air which was quite alarming. She had a long, thin key, slung at her girdle; there was a grating sound in her voice; her lips were compressed, and when she kissed him, as her custom was, twice, she startled him by saying that she had given out all he could have for two days. It gradually dawned upon him that the new régime, ushered in by the early morning bell, included an entire reorganization of the establishment, and that all supplies were being doled out by the exact quantity. The household had been put upon rations, and what was not by weight was to be by measure. Like a wise prince, as he was, he forbore any protest or objection, having, during the day, felt a little ashamed of his heartlessness in the matter of the bell.

The Little Lady was thus left without obstruction in the pathway of reform. The only drawback to the new system of the giving out of supplies was that her pound was a very variable quantity. Sometimes, it corresponded to our troy weight, and sometimes, it was avoirdupois, and sometimes, it

was of a standard entirely her own, wholly unrec-
ognized by custom or statute. She did her best,
however, to keep her hand steady and her scales
true, and to dispense her stores according to a just
economy, affecting to disregard all the signs of dis-
pleasure and disgust, which, like lowering clouds,
betokened a coming storm.

Domesticus knew perfectly well how to out-
manœuvre and out-general the Little Lady, and,
after amusing himself for some time by causing her
to be interrupted in every conversation, wakening
her out of every afternoon nap, startling her at the
moment of seating herself at the table, and even
breaking in upon her most sacred moments of
privacy, with demands for things she had forgotten
to give out, or which some unexpected emergency
required to be doubled in quantity, he marshaled
his forces for a mutinous revolt. Possibly the
weights and measures might have been tolerated
for a longer period, but the too punctual ringing of
the bell, which as the clock struck the hour of ten
at night, like the curfew of William the Conqueror,
tolled the knell of parting for the lingering followers, below stairs, was beyond endurance.

One fine morning, the Prince found himself at his
breakfast table without a drop of coffee, or a morsel
of bread, or a pat of butter. There was no sugar, no
milk, no syrup for possible cakes, no salt for expected
eggs; in place of the accustomed chop, there was
an empty platter; and worse than all, there was no
explanation, but only ominous and foreboding

silence. Finally, upon compulsion, the declaration
was extorted that there was nothing eatable in the
house, outside of the store-room. The **Little Lady**
appeared, in all the loveliness of **her early morning**
attire, and her **eye** took in the situation **at once.**
She had given out all the needed supplies **for the**
day, with the liberality **of a** Princess, heaped up,
pressed down, and running over, but they had been
secretly, **or** surreptitiously, kept **back,** and now the
**pretended** deficiency was to **be** laid at **her door, and**
she must surrender her **key, or** her **empire would**
be in revolt. Surrender she would not. But the
Prince must have his breakfast, and a salt-cellar
without salt was something **not to be tolerated for a**
moment. She said not a **word, but descended with**
an unfaltering step into the arena. The insurgents
**were** prepared for her coming. The whole stock
of supplies had been diverted by their connivance,
and she **was to** be starved into submission. In the
pause **which** followed her appearing, the combined
charge was made. **She was no lady;** no decent person could **live with the likes of her;** all the household divinities **were invoked against her** stinginess,
and the ultimatum was announced—the **key must**
be delivered up as the price of **peace.**

The Princess stood firm; **she** charged back upon
**the mutineers** their treachery and **treason; the**
combat thickened; **the** Prince descended in alarm;
**the** tumult raged, **and when order was at** last
restored, **and the** Little Lady, **who** had maintained
her position **to the end,** declared that **she** would

proceed to the store-room, and give out the things
for a breakfast which must be prepared on the
instant, she discovered, to her dismay and confusion, on putting her hand to her girdle, that the
key was gone. Whether she had mislaid it by
accident, or whether, by some artful trick or device
of Domesticus, it had been spirited away into the
limbo of lost things, will never be known. It could
not be found; resort was had to violence; the store-
room door was forced and the wants of the household supplied.

With that breaking in, although never acknowledged by the Little Lady, the whole short-
lived system of weights and measures, and daily
dispensations was broken up. There was delay
in adjusting a new lock. The substituted key,
somehow, would not cling to her dainty waist.
The way to the store-room seemed longer. The
door was oftener left open. By degrees, the ringing
of the curfew became a neglected duty, and one
morning, when the Little Lady started from her
slumbers, to find the hour long past when she
ought to have sounded the awakening alarm, as she
pulled the silken cord, with sudden force, it gave
way, broke at the ceiling, and falling upon her neck,
and shoulders, and slender form, encircled her like
the coils of a serpent.

It was never replaced.

# CHAPTER VI.

## DOMESTICUS AND THE CHILDREN.

THE Upas tree which Domesticus had planted in the Little Lady's bower of bliss, whose roots were underneath the foundation, and whose branches overshadowed the roof, bore some of its deadliest fruit in the Nursery. As the palace, in due time, was occupied by new comers it was painful to see how they would get into the grasp of Domesticus as soon as they were born. He lay in wait for them, like an Ogre of the old school. The first little princess was the special victim of his devices. The Little Lady considered that what her new maternity most lacked was experience, and Domesticus undertook to supply the deficiency in the guise of an elderly female who had been the mother of thirteen children. It was soon apparent that she regarded herself as charged with the care of two infants, instead of one, and that mother and babe were equally subject to her sway. Her experience was like the stream of Time. It began in a remote past, and meandered, through long intermediate periods, down to the moment of her present service. It bore on its bosom the undisclosed secrets and the hidden scandals of many generations. In the

43

abstract, it embraced everything within the compass of human affairs; in the concrete, it was mainly conversant with catnip tea, paregoric, and pins. It must be remembered that, at the time of the birth of the Princess Prima, for this was her name, neither the telephone, the electric light, nor the safety pin, were known to the inventive arts in Magna Patria, if indeed they are known there to this day; and that the culling of such simples as catnip, and the mixing of such draughts as paregoric, were part and parcel of the orthodox cruelties practiced upon helpless infancy. To these inflictions Domesticus lent a ready and willing hand. Dean Swift's famous plan for preventing the increase of population in Ireland, by the systematic slaughter of all Irish babies, which was only one of his many huge, coarse jokes, would at all times have been dead earnest to Domesticus. Why else did he envelop each new-born member of the human family in layer upon layer, and fold upon fold, of impervious material, making the hapless victim more fit for the companionship of mummies than of mammas? Why else persist in covering up its tiny breathing apparatus, so as to make its incipient efforts at respiration almost impossible of success, and so as to induce apoplexy in the infant of a day? Why else persist in excluding the free, fresh air of heaven, as an element unfriendly to a child of earth? Why else persist in forcing into its thimble-sized stomach five times the volume of fluid it could contain, and then subject it to the never-ending, still-beginning trot, on inelastic knees, such as those of the little Prima's dry nurse Experientia?

Meanwhile, in spite of Domesticus, the fair floweret grew on, in a natural, healthy way of its own, resisting these baneful influences with all the miniature forces with which Nature had endowed her. But to no purpose. At every outcry, Domesticus was ready with a fiction, founded, only too truly, on fact. The little darling was abused, so it was, everybody abused it, so they did, and it must have some catnip. Thus was poison poured into the ear of earliest infancy, while poison was being poured down its throat, and as the imagined occasions of abuse multiplied, so did the catnip increase in quantity and strength, the doses of paregoric became more potent, and the pins more frequent. The young Princess struggled and fought, with all the feeble might of her legs and lungs, and made night and day, by turns, hideous with her protests, but the infant Hercules himself could not have strangled the serpent Domesticus if he had crawled into his cradle. The previous question of the morning, the subsequent question of the evening, and the intermediate question of the day, was very apt to be, " What makes that child cry?"

" It is because she is abused, she is," said Experientia.

" I fear it is total depravity," said the Prince.

" I believe it is pins," said the Little Lady.

And, on a careful investigation it generally proved to be pins.

Thereupon, after a time, pins were proscribed; and Prima and the succeeding little prince and princess were sewed up every morning, and ripped up every night, and worked over and over, like old time samplers, until they had stitches in their sides, and their backs, and all over.

But the Little Lady, to whom the new heart throbs, which began when she felt the first touch of Prima's velvet cheek upon her breast, were a fresh inspiration, only waited to recruit her strength, in order to rally all the forces of instinct and affection to the defence of her offspring. Windows were thrown open, flannels were torn off, the vile mixtures went to the ash-heap, and Prima's little bare pink legs, and arms, and breast, and back, were bathed in sunshine and pure air, as freely as in the tempered waters of the bath, or in the overflowing fountain of maternal love. Here, in a double sense, was a new life for the Princess. The fresh existence, whose tiny tendrils reached forth to draw support and sustenance from her own life, seemed to have its counterpart in the responsive tenderness of her sustaining and protecting love, so different from any earlier feeling, so transcendent and unique; at first, the simplest instinct groping in the dark and the dawn, but how soon expanding, until in its all-embracing care, it seemed a second Providence in the sphere of home.

One thing was certain: Domesticus should not come between her and her children. Sooner than have them gobbled up by this arch destroyer, she

would devour them herself, as did Saturn. She
would do all the washing, and dressing, and undress-
ing, and putting to sleep, and waking up. No voice
but her own should soothe or chide ; no hand but
her's caress or correct. Alas ! the delegation to
Domesticus, at least in part, was only too soon a dire
necessity. The papoose of the Imperial City will
not submit to being suspended from a bracket, or
borne on the back, while the daily round of maternal duties is being performed. Neither the prime-
val forest, nor the aboriginal methods of Magna
Patria, could find place within metropolitan limits.
Civilization was the ally of Domesticus.

But the Princess was determined not to be entangled again in the meshes of any experience except
her own, and in her efforts at maternal independence she went from one extreme to another ; from
the wisdom of the herb-mixing ancient to the
unwisdom personified in one of those youthful
forms, with pendent braids, and high-necked aprons,
whom Domesticus sent forth, duly commissioned
to mind children, and carefully instructed not to
mind their parents. Divers specific rules and
regulations he imparted, besides, out of sheer mal-
evolence. The child, if propelled in a miniature
chariot, should always be stopped under the full
blaze of the sun, while the propelling attendant
exchanged views, on topics of common interest,
with other propellers. The child when able to
walk, should be jerked over gutters and along side-
walks, by the hand, so that the mechanical power,

gained by the leverage of the arm, might be
brought to bear upon the entire frame, in aid of its
permanent distortion and dislocation. Excursions
to remote places, in the social interest of Domesticus; surreptitious supplies of indigestible sweets;
threatenings of swift and awful retribution in case
of disclosure of any doubtful doings of Domesticus; the peopling of the dark with monsters
and hobgoblins; the investing even of innocent
ragpickers and sweeps with supposed diabolism
towards the entire infant population of the globe—
are only samples of these special, unsealed instructions.

Nevertheless, the Little Lady's vigilance, though
sorely taxed, was never intermitted. Her mother-
liness was always at the meridian. It was radiant
with all the brightness of her nature, and it had a
potency which was irresistible. So it happened
that the wiles of Domesticus were held in check,
and most of the mischief he plotted against the
children came to naught, and in spite of the many
trials and many failures of the struggle, there were
some bright memories of loving and faithful service
to the little ones, from hands and hearts, which,
though under the original jurisdiction of Domesticus, and owing native allegiance to him, were so
naturalized in the special domain of home that they
came to share its sacred associations and affections.
This was a part of the open reward of mother-love
which so often can be seen only in secret. What
watchings were hers through long nights of suffer-

ing, made so much harder for the watcher because the little sufferer could not describe or declare its needs, except by cry, or moan, or convulsive movement; what patient waiting, alike in hope or fear, for the dreaded, or impatiently expected crisis, of disease; what bearing of all the myriad burdens which childhood in its thoughtless, or perverse, or, far oftener, its undisciplined, or unsound, condition, puts upon the parental heart; and what never ceasing care, carried in its inmost core, by day and by night, at home, abroad and everywhere.

She was never separated from the children by sea or land, rarely was she beyond call, never did she leave them a moment for any pleasure at the cost of duty. And so they grew, under her eye, and hand, and heart, and the little Prima, the firstling of the flock, soon expanded into rare beauty, and loveliness, which were shared by a sister and brother who came, in time, to be her playmates.

The Prince was of very little use in the care or training of the children. If they were little ailing, he thought they were very ill. If they were very ill, he thought they were going to die. He would misapprehend colic for temper. He thought four o'clock in the morning an unreasonable hour for a frolic with a wide-awake baby. He soon tired of protracted vigils and the walking up and down, in the small hours of the night, with the small occupant of his arms persistently bent on keeping as many members of the family, as possible, astir and out of bed. He was too strict; he was too indulgent; he

4

corrected too harshly; he punished injudiciously; he forgave without waiting for due penitence; he allowed prohibited things; he proposed impossible projects; he made irredeemable promises; he did his best to spoil the whole brood, but he never interfered with the reign of the Queen-mother, and in this, he shewed himself a discerning Prince, whose example is to be commended to all fathers who fancy there can be two sovereigns in the same empire, or any substitute, in love or law, for a mother's heart, or a mother's care.

# CHAPTER VII.

## DOMESTICUS AFRICANUS.

IF I have omitted, thus far, any mention of that prime factor in the forces of the enemy with whom the Little Lady was waging her weary war, Domesticus Africanus, it is because his importance requires a special and separate treatment. His dark shadow fell across the path of our Princess at an early point of her progress. The ineradicable hostility of Domesticus Hibernicus to this dusky co-worker in the sphere of household service was something which had often proved an explosive fire-damp in her subterranean quarters. Domesticus Africanus was an exotic which could not thrive unless in company with a kindred stock. His presence was a sure signal of disturbance, especially at meal times, below stairs, as Domesticus Hibernicus drew the line of non-intercourse just where Shylock drew his, in his relations with the Venetian Gentiles; he would wait with him, wash with him, scrub with him, gossip with him, but he would not eat with him. The pre-eminent social qualities of Domesticus Africanus in his native circles were perennial sources of disorder in the domain of duty; his adaptation for elegant leisure was a continuously demoralizing element, and his religious enthusiasm was too exalted in its vocal pitch for the precincts of a palace, and too absorbing in its requirements for the routine of daily work.

Besides all this, at the period in the history of Magna Patria at which my story has now arrived, Domesticus Africanus was assuming an importance that was overshadowing and supreme. He was not indigenous to that fair realm, nor had he come of his own will, from beyond seas, to its shores. As my readers may all have learned, long ago, Magna Patria is a cluster of sister sovereignties, born, after agonizing birth-throes, into the family of the nations, and bound together by a compact, meant to be firm enough to keep them all under a common rule; elastic enough to leave them all free to rule themselves within their separate and several bounds; and broad enough to open and let in new and equal members of the Sisterhood, as vacant spaces of the fair realm should be occupied.

Brought, as a captive, from his native tropics, Domesticus Africanus had been held in bondage, throughout the Sisterhood, until, in course of time in those parts of it where his labor was not especially required, because the zone was so tempered that no man was driven by the sun from his mid-day work, he was suffered to go free and of his own will to work, or not work,—which was often more to his taste,—whereas in those parts where labor must be under a torrid heat, which he alone could best endure, he was kept enslaved.

And thus it came about that an invisible line was drawn across the fair land of the Sisterhood, on the nether side of which Domesticus Africanus was a thing, and a chattel, and was bought and sold, and on the upper side of which he was a man and a person and so, if being on the nether side, he could contrive to get to the upper side and stay there, a magical change was instantly wrought in him, whereby he became a person, instead of a thing, and belonged to himself, instead of the master or mistress whom he had left behind.  But he was always liable to be pursued, and captured, and sent back, because it was a part of the compact of the Sisterhood that every such runaway might lawfully, be caught and reclaimed, and in such case, be delivered up, like any other stray animal, on proof of property, to the rightful owner, and thereupon become once more, and immediately, a thing and not a person.

It was quite otherwise, however, if his master or mistress happened to bring Domesticus Africanus across the invisible line, and while on the upper side, he could contrive to get away from them, because then they might not reclaim him, but the magical change was a permanent one, and he became a person, and belonged to himself, by a free and absolute title.  These arrangements were so complicated that Domesticus Africanus was a long while in coming to any definite understanding of the possible conditions under which he might cease to be a thing, and become a person; and he was, in the main, well satisfied to be and remain a thing, and not to become a person, so long as he did not know the difference, and nobody told him.

It is easy to see that as Domesticus Africanus grew and multiplied on the nether side of the invisible line, and his progeny came to be counted by the million, and all these were property, just as much as the cattle on the hills, or the crops in the fields, the good people who possessed all this property, which constituted the main part of their wealth, and who believed in their hearts that it was a part of the duly established order of created things that they should have and enjoy their own, naturally came to be very jealous of any interference with their rights. In their eyes, the holding of Domesticus Africanus in bondage was an Institution, and, by and by, a great many of them began to think, and to assert, that it was a divine Institution, to be upheld and perpetuated by all possible means, and this not only in their own selfish interest, but for the well-being of Domesticus Africanus. He could not thrive, they claimed, by himself, but must be under guardianship, and pupilage, and government. A child of the tropics, he must be kept in the glow and warmth of the sunshine, and being inclined by his nature to bask in it, in idleness, he must be made to labor, for his own good, and his service should be gratuitous, as a due return for the protection and nurture he received, and for which the devotion of a life-time was only a fair equivalent.

Accordingly, they were greatly indignant against the good people who, living on the upper side of the invisible line, where there was no ownership in Domesticus Africanus, claimed and insisted that he ought, everywhere, to be a person and not a thing; and that to own him, or hold him, or buy him, or sell him, was a wrong and a crime. The people of this way of thinking hated the invisible line, although they could no more abolish it than they could wipe out the Equator. They hated the Institution, which so far from being divine, they declared to be of the Devil. They hated the compact, which made it possible to transform Domesticus Africanus into a thing after he had once chosen to be a person, and made his choice effectual by getting to the upper side of the line. Carrying these ideas into execution, they devised ways and means by which, if Domesticus Africanus was once so lucky as to get both feet across the line, he could, either above ground or under ground, be caught up and spirited away, beyond reach of pursuers, or possibility of capture. They raised a great outcry against the Institution; they declared that it ought to be abolished, and cut up, root and branch, and were so loud and violent that they came, in their turn, to be hated and dreaded by the whole of the Sisterhood on the nether side of the invisible line, as much as they themselves hated the Institution.

So, in the nature of things, a conflict was inevitable. More and more, the good people to whom Domesticus Africanus was a thing, and not a person, became alienated from the good people to whom he was a person, and not a thing. They tried, by every means, to protect themselves against spoliation, but their riches were of a kind very apt to take to themselves legs and run away. In vain did they stop the ears of Domesticus Africanus, so that he should not hear the outcry; in vain did they blindfold his eyes and shackle his limbs, so that he could not find his way, if he would, across the invisible line. He became a perpetual source of discord and disturbance. No one was permitted to teach him to read, or to write, or to think, and yet, in spite of all these precautions, nothing was more common than that he would scamper off and get over the line, and then it would be a world of trouble to catch him and get him back, and very often, he was never caught or got back, but was an absolutely lost thing to his master or mistress.

It gradually became more and more hazardous for the good people of Netherdom to come, even for a season, to the upper side of the invisible line, with so much as a single specimen of Domesticus Africanus in their train, because of the keen scent which the Abolishers, as they were called, had for this species of game, and their many expert ways of bagging it, in its own interest, to the utter extinction of all pre-existing rights of property.

All this was exceedingly aggravating, and the wisest and shrewdest of the good people with whom the Institution was the corner stone of their social fabric, came to see, clearly, that unless by their own efforts, and with the help of their fellows on the upper side of the line who were not in accord with the Abolishers, they could gain and keep the ascendency in the Sisterhood, they would always be at a disadvantage, and the Institution would be in constant and increasing danger. They must rule or be ruined.

Thus they were, of necessity, from their point of view, unable and unwilling to let bad enough alone. They must needs make things worse, by desperately claiming and proclaiming that the Institution was a vital element, to grow with the growth and strengthen with the strength of the fair land of the Sisterhood, lest the just equilibrium between its various members should be disturbed. And whenever new domains came to be added, and the old boundaries were enlarged to take in broad areas, where there were no lines, visible or invisible, they insisted that the Institution should be set up wherever they chose to plant it, and make it grow in the virgin soil of these new parts and places. But to this the good people of the upper side of the invisible line would not agree. In the main, they were willing enough to abide by the compact, and not to meddle with the Institution, or with Domesticus Africanus. They were even willing to aid in silencing the outcry against them, and in suppressing the obnoxious

Abolishers, and multiplying the ways and means by which the compact as to the fugitives should be made effectual, and to bring out shot-guns and soldiers, if need be, to make sure the capture and return of any stray chattel who, in the effort surreptitiously to become a person, had been seized by his owner and must be relegated to serfdom.

All this seemed right and just or, at least, necessary, however it might shock some sensibilities and go counter to some consciences; but here the line of concession was drawn, and while the compact must be kept, and the Institution tolerated where it existed, not a foot, nor an inch, of new ground should be yielded to it. It should be kept penned and chained within the limits where it belonged, as its victims were sometimes penned and chained by their taskmasters; and it should be girdled round with fire, until it worked out its own destruction and stung itself to death. And this was a new and growing grievance, and prolific source of discontent to the masters and mistresses of Domesticus Africanus.

On both sides of the invisible line, some things were forgotten. On the upper side, they forgot that the Institution had, aforetime, been a part of their own social system, and that it had ceased to exist with them, not altogether because the fathers on that side of the line were any more virtuous or just than their fellow-men, but because they did not need it any longer. On the nether side, they forgot that the fathers of the Sisterhood never meant that the Institution should remain as a permanent thing, to become a dominating power, but only to be endured as an evil, at some time to cease; and, especially, they forgot that there were restless spirits at work, the world over, sweeping away all institutions, and wiping out all lines which hindered the human race in the pathway cleared for it by that mighty and mysterious power which men call Progress.

The good people of the nether side, being all of one accord about the Institution, made the further great mistake of supposing that the good people of the upper side, except the obnoxious Abolishers, were so busy, tilling their acres, sailing their ships, twirling their spindles, building their houses, selling their wares, and otherwise getting gain, that they would be quite indifferent about the matter, and ready to submit to almost any sacrifice, rather than to provoke a serious disturbance about the Institution. In this confidence they went on, waxing more and more persistent and violent, until they openly declared, that unless they could be protected in all their rights as they claimed them, they would no longer remain in the Sisterhood, but would go out from it, and be no more a part of it, and would confederate among themselves as a separate people, so as by all means to save the Institution—all of which seemed idle threats to the good people of the upper side.

Meanwhile, slowly and surely, the foundations had been laid of a new power, strong and resolute to maintain, in their integrity, the ancient landmarks the Fathers had set, and to resist, by all means, within the compact, the baleful forces which threatened to destroy the unity of the Sisterhood. It gained the ascendant at the very crisis of the Nation's fate. In the person of its chosen leader, it gave a new name to the roll of the world's martyrs and emancipators. It knit the hearts of all loyal Union-loving men, as the heart of one man, in the long, dark struggle. It won for itself the right to this simple word of praise, that as the faithful servant of the Sisterhood, it saved—albeit at a great price— the birthright of Freedom which no mad endeavor could destroy.

# CHAPTER VIII.

## THE STRIFE OF THE SISTERHOOD.

AS we are not concerned so much with the fortunes of the Sisterhood, as with those of one of its lowly and lovely daughters, it is needless to trace, in detail, the story of this discordant time. Suffice it to say, that the outcome of the discord was a season of hideous ruin and combustion dire. A firebrand from the upper side was flung into the nether side, by a wild, frenzied onslaught, within its borders; the lawless outburst of a handful of enthusiasts numbering less than a score of men, under a leader whose lifeless body soon dangled from a felon's gibbet, in expiation of his crime, but whose name, caught up and resounded on a million lips, became a battle cry, the like of which was never heard before among the sons of men.

Firebrands from the nether side were soon flying, thick and fast. One after another, the sisters below the invisible line cast off the compact, and declared themselves quit of its obligations. At last, one April morning, where, over a wave-washed rampart, far off on the nether side, a bit of bunting, bearing a star-sprinkled patch of blue, and streaked with alternate stripes of white and red, was fluttering in

61

the early breeze, a puff of white smoke rose in mid-air, landward, and a cannon shot was fired, with deadly aim, upon the dingy, wind-worn symbol of the union and sovereignty of the Sisterhood. A single shot, but its sudden, sharp concussion dislodged the avalanche of War, as, in the high Alps, the chance discharge of a huntsman's rifle loosens the long suspended, tottering masses of snow and ice, and hurls them down the mountain's shattered side, with ruin in their track.

A single shot; but it summoned the whole Sisterhood to arms, on the one side to sever it in twain, on the other side to save it alive in its unity. It startled, and wakened out of their fancied security, the sleepers and dreamers on both sides of the invisible line. It splintered, and shattered, and crushed out of shape, old expedients, and pretexts, and subterfuges, and made many a refuge of lies as unsafe a shelter as a tall tree in a thunder storm. It opened a clear, wide space, through which, as if a rift had been cut into the heavens, was seen in a new light, what was true, and right, and needful, to be done and suffered, and in which it was revealed that, on both sides of the line, men were made of such stuff that they would rather die than submit to what, in heart and conscience, they thought was wrong.

And so the good fight to save the Sisterhood began, and went on, drenching the fair land with blood, filling its homes with mourning, furrowing its soil with the graves of heroes, but welding, in

its furnace fires, a new and purer Sovereignty, to be
divided no more by separating lines, and sullied no
longer by the dark stain which was the source of
all the baleful strife.

At first, it was intended by the good people of
the upper side of the invisible line that the war
which they never thought of beginning, but at last
were driven to undertake, should be waged wholly
without reference to the question of Domesticus
Africanus, or the Institution. The Sisterhood was
to be saved from disruption and restored without change. The cancer-eaten body was to be
cured, without touching the cancer. The Ship of
State was to be got safely to Tarshish with Jonah
under the hatches. The Institution, which had
made all the mischief, was not to be meddled with.
The separating sisters were to be constrained at the
cannon's mouth, and pressed with the point of the
bayonet, to come back, just as they were, before
that fateful shot was fired. This was the wisdom of
the wisest who waged the war, and they undertook
to deal with Domesticus Africanus as if there were,
in reality, no war, and as if all the slaughter, on both
sides, were simply to settle the vexed question
whether or not the Sisterhood could be broken up,
at will, by any of the separate sisters.

Accordingly when, under cover of the hubbub of
the marching, and countermarching, and attack, and
invasion, Domesticus Africanus came straggling,
now and then, within the camp lines of the invaders, having got through his thick skull a faint

notion that, in some way, he was concerned in the fight, and that it might be better for him to steal away from the encircling arms of the Institution than to abide where he was, he was courteously sent back, by the invaders, to his master or mistress, by order of the wise men. But presently, there came to be a foolishness wiser than this wisdom. If Domesticus Africanus was property on the nether side of the line, and if the invaders were waging a real war, and were actual and not make believe belligerents, and entitled by all the rules of war, to use and confiscate the property of the enemy, why was not Domesticus Africanus, when found within the invaders' lines, lawful prize, as contraband of war? He could not be reclaimed by his former owner, under the compact, because the compact was broken by the owner and sought to be utterly destroyed, and as, in the eyes of the invaders, the property was of a description that belonged to itself, he came to a kind of intermediate state, between being a thing and being a person, and, for the time being, was labelled " Domesticus Contrabandus."

It was at this precise point that our good Prince was sorely puzzled and perplexed. In common with a great many of his fellow princes of the Imperial City, he had clung to the hope, first, that the Sisterhood could be saved without a fight, and then, that if a fight were inevitable, it could go on without harming the Institution. He was well satisfied with things as they were. He had lively sympathies with Netherdom. A tenth cousin of his maternal grandfather, had at some remote period of time, settled and married in that sunny clime, and had become a participant in the benefits of the Institution. Such a tie, however slender in fact, was of a wonderful potency in sentiment and sympathy; and was supposed to create a kind of secret pledge and hypothecation of the opinion and conscience of the most distant collateral connections on the upper side of the line, by way of security for the inviolability of the Institution. The Prince had been often on the nether side, and had been entertained there, as became his princely rank, returning home, after each successive visit, with glowing accounts of what he had seen and enjoyed.

Most of his experiences had been prior to his marriage, but many a heartache had he given the Little Lady, all unconsciously, as he dilated upon the liberal and patriarchal hospitalities of which his memory retained a vivid impression, and to which he was fond of recurring. There, Domesticus was born and brought up in the bosom of the Family, and was bound, by the sacred tie of property, to a life-long, loyal service. The Institution, seen from this bright side, was like a tree of life in the midst of a garden. It made possible, in reality, what he had only dreamed of, in vision, or read about in romance. Houses wide open; tables spread daily and with lavish bounty, for troops of guests, expected or unexpected; viands supplied from the abundant resources at hand, requiring nothing exotic to add to their excellence, and of which, in

5

their wonderful preparation, the secrets were hereditary and were part of the traditions of a family and a race; and all this ruled over with a kind of paternal and feudal sway, by models of manly daring and womanly grace, undisturbed by the fretting cares of petty routine, or by the wearisome change and worrying friction of the life at home.

"After all," said the Princess, when the Prince would pause, after one of his high-wrought descriptions, "no wonder they can be hospitable, when they can command work without wages, and own the people who do it. If we could buy and sell Domesticus as we pleased, or raise him and grow him, like corn and cabbages, we could be just as hospitable, and entertain just as well, possibly better, than they do. But what right have they got to own Domesticus Africanus and make him do their work for nothing?"

Then the Prince would explain to her that Domesticus Africanus was under a special, old time curse and ban, which bound him, and his posterity, to fetch and carry forever. Also, that the Institution was a great blessing to him and his children, because it provided them with homes, and food, and raiment, and other necessaries of life, having which they ought to be content.

"I can't see," said the Princess, "how you can make out a thing to be a curse and a blessing at the same time, or when it stops being a curse and begins being a blessing. The long and the short of it is that they get the work and give no pay. A great many of the emissaries of Domesticus, hereabouts, may be under a curse—they act as if they were—plenty of them—but nobody kidnaps them and makes them work for nothing."

"What can these good people do?" said the Prince. "They have got Domesticus Africanus on their hands and they must keep him."

"That doesn't hinder their paying him and letting him feel that he is a man."

"He is paid, in food, and clothing, and care."

"So are dogs, and horses, and oxen, fed and cared for, but is he not much better than they?"

Then the Prince would explain that, in a certain sense, he was, and, again, in a certain other sense, he was not, and the Princess would urge that he had a soul as well as a body, and press the point, until the Prince would admit, with some qualifications, that he had a soul, but of an altogether inferior, and so to speak, unmarketable quality and grade, in fact, a damaged article, the whole race bring a kind of job lot, very far below the average social standard, and doomed to perpetual degradation.

"Of course," she would say, indignantly, "if it is to be perpetually degraded; but it does seem to me against nature, and against right, and against conscience, for a man to claim to own another man."

This always led the Prince to say, very solemnly, that there were a great many excellent, wise and superior men, who believed in the Institution and its divine character, and that circumstances altered cases, in the matter of souls, and bodies, and races, as well as in respect to other things, and that, on the whole, Domesticus Africanus was far better off as he was than if he were roaming about in his native nakedness, with wild beasts, in jungles and forests, and that the meddlesome Abolishers were doing infinite mischief, by stirring up questions which only made trouble, and that they were un-settling the foundations, and if the foundations were destroyed what would become of the Merchant Princes?

This idea of danger to the foundations was a source of constant alarm to the Prince and his fellows, as it involved the undermining, to a very large extent, of the whole system of Dry Goods, and the possible loss of millions of uncounted sestertia. War was the very last thing they wanted and even when they found themselves enveloped in its murky cloud, and saw its grim shape, stalking, like a fiend, across their path, they were still con-sulting the oracles, and inspecting the omens and crying "Peace, peace," until, in the midst of their vociferations and expostulations, the whirlwind rose, and the storm burst, and the lightnings flashed, and the floods came, and the foundations were swept away, and the Institution was hurled, as by an aveng-ing Almighty hand, into the blackness of darkness forever.

# CHAPTER IX.

## COMING AND GOING OF CONTRABANDUS.

IT was before this final and blessed consummation had been reached, and while the good fight was in its earlier stages, the Prince, in his wisdom, being still sorely perplexed with the problem of how to save the Sisterhood, without hurting the Institution, and Domesticus Africanus, in his unwisdom, being more sorely perplexed to comprehend his anomalous predicament of being neither a thing nor a person, but only a contraband of war, that a new and surprising piece of information was communicated to the Little Lady. The Prince, one evening, with an air of supreme self satisfaction, announced that the home problem was about to receive a partial, if not a perfect solution, in the person of Domesticus Contrabandus, whom their household was to receive on the morrow.

It had come about in this wise: Domesticus Africanus, was, as far as his opportunities permitted, on the move, in the invaded regions, towards the pickets of the invaders. From all that was going on below the invisible line, he appeared to be drawing the inference that he could become a person. This inference was very often drawn with the aid of a horse and cart, which being the property of his master or mistress, was, in the existing state of war, equally contraband with himself, and forfeited to the enemy by all the usages of contending powers. So, in good conscience, and as an act of authorized hostility, he would pile into the cart, under cover of the night, all his contraband belongings, consisting of his wife, and children, or as many of them as had not been sold away from him, and such other movables as were within convenient reach, and depart from the house of bondage, without stopping to shake off the dust from his feet. The contrabands, who thus flocked into the lines of the invaders, were set to doing camp drudgery, and many of them were disposed of in such manner that they could begin, at once, to try the experiment of being persons, on their own account.

In the course of such dispositions, a brave warrior, commanding in the ranks of the invaders, of kin to our Prince, consigned to him the particular specimen of the new genus Contrabandus, of whose coming the Princess was apprised. It was a cheering anticipation. She was given to understand that she was now about to appreciate the blessings of the Institution, without becoming a sharer in its crimes. She would have the skilled and trained services of Domesticus Africanus, with the privilege of paying him, at the market rate, for the labor he performed. She could teach him to read, and write, and cipher, and think, and elevate him, as high as she pleased, in the scale of humanity. The Prince was delighted at this lucky stroke, in which philanthropy, political economy, and social progress seemed to be happily combined, and while the Princess was not without some secret misgivings as to the result, she awaited, with mingled hope and apprehension, the coming of the Atlas who was to lift the load from her weary shoulders.

The morrow came, and with it, came Contrabandus. Having achieved his personal freedom, he considered himself equal to any possible emergency, and took immediate possession of the palace, as if coming into a patrimony of which he was the rightful heir. Fresh from the din and stir of contending armies, and the excitement of camp life, his general demeanor was that of a belligerent, ready to lead, or follow, in any forlorn hope. There was not a ray of encouragement for the Princess in any of the inky lines of his Ethiopic face, nor a redeeming touch to its ugliness, save that at every parting of the vastness of his lips he disclosed a set of ivories which, in spite of her horror at the thought of owning a fellow being, in whole or in part, the Princess wished she could buy and reduce to immediate possession. However, if she could, for a little season, suspend her daily anxiety in regard to the department in which he was to exercise his supposed skill and experience, she would become accustomed to his unsightly aspect, and there was solid comfort in his teeth.

The Prince, who believed with Macbeth that "the sauce to meat is ceremony," deemed himself fortu-

nate in being able to signalize the inauguration of
the new era in his household administration by the
presence, at his board, of a select company, who
would be made doubly at their case by the ministrations of Contrabandus. He came home, a little
in advance of his expected guests, and as he entered
his palace, now in the safe custody of the newly in-
stalled Major-domo, his sense of smell was saluted
by an all-pervading odor which he instantly asso-
ciated with the means by which the houses of the
Imperial City were illuminated at night. It was in
the grand hall, on the staircase, and in full possession of the mansion, though, as yet, unperceived by
the Princess, who was enveloped in the mysteries of
her toilette. The Prince raised the hue and cry,
customary with householders in such cases of escape,
but after long search, no unclosed outlet was discovered.

Suddenly, a suspicion crossed the mind of the
Prince.

" Where is Contrabandus ? "

He was found by the Prince, who on receiving
an intimation as to his probable whereabouts, went
in swift search of him, in the outer court, at the rear
of the palace, engaged in the act of dealing tremendous blows upon the side of a barrel which he was
vainly endeavoring to open by splitting it in the
centre, as if it were an immense section of a felled
tree.

" What are you about ? " asked the Prince.

" Performin' on dish yer bar'l " replied Contrabandus, resting from his labors and displaying his ivories.

"Leave the barrel alone and answer me this question—did you put out the light in the cellarium?"

"Yes, massa, blowed her out clean—had to blow bustin' hard, but blowed her out—never performed on a light like dat afore."

The Prince recalled a tradition that, when a noted hero of the nether side of the line, a master of the arts of eloquence, a leader of the Senate of Magna Patria, and once a candidate for her highest civic honor, made his first visit to the Imperial City, he was reported to have nearly lost his life by asphyxia, induced by his "performing," in the same way, upon the aerial light in his apartment, while spending the night in the mansion of a friend. Held in check, by this memory, from seizing the hatchet and decapitating Contrabandus on the spot, he good naturedly conducted him to the subterranean place of his offence, and gave him an object lesson in the science of Illumination.

To complete this special course of instruction, he then took him to the banqueting hall, to initiate him, at once, into the higher branches of the art. With his own princely hand he lighted the tiny instrument of ignition, by a slight friction of its inflammable point on the rough surface of the receptacle from which he took it, and then went through the equally familiar process of illuminating, with its aid, some of the light-diffusing jets, pendent over the table, already decorated for the coming repast. Contrabandus obeyed the injunction to follow the process at every advancing step, in order to its immediate imitation, testifying his admiration in a series of exclamations, in a loud key, as if intended to attract the attention of distant spectators in the outer air.

"Stop that shouting, Contrabandus," said the Prince. "Now take the box and light that wall bracket yourself."

Contrabandus seized, not only the proffered box, but also the half consumed stump, which the Prince still held in his hand, and with a frantic gesture, described, with its sooty point, a long line of black, across the pearl-tinted panel from which the bracket projected.

"Reckon dish yer lucifer is w'at you teched off afore, Massa," said Contrabandus, reckless of the damage he had done, but with genuine surprise at the failure of his experiment, and its result in evoking darkness instead of light.

The Prince stood aghast. He surveyed Contrabandus from head to foot. There were divisions of labor on the lower side of the line, as well defined and thoroughly regulated as in the realms of hired service. To what had he been born and bred?

"Contrabandus," said the Prince, in his most princely tone, "have you ever waited at table?"

"Reckon I has, Massa—on forty to wunst—O go 'long 'bout waitin'—clar'd de track dat time and got de dishes in 'head of everybody."

This was literally true. Once in his life, and but

once, had Contrabandus waited at table, and on
forty guests. It was at a barbecue, in a pine grove;
for Contrabandus was a field hand, and conversant
with cattle from his youth.

The Prince had to dress for dinner and he could
not linger. Heavy of heart, and with dire forebodings, he turned to leave the room, but tarried an
instant for a query too important to omit.

" Is the Falernian in the ice ? "

" Oh, yes, Massa—out of all dose yer long-necked
flagons. De Missus she told me to put it in ice
and I'se got it all out—had to chop off de necks
—reckon dey got twisted up somehow with wires
—chopped 'em clean off wid de hatchet, and dey
kinder flew like, but cotched de most of it and no
glass in de tub."

" Tub ! " echoed the Prince in dismay.

" Yes, Massa, all out in one tub—de teetotal
dozen and chunks of ice to boot—all ready for
dippin' out."

The Prince gave one long deep groan and vanished. It was not that the whole case of extra dry
Falernian, which he had sent home for judicious
testing, by expert palates, had been sacked and ex-
terminated by the rude hand of Contrabandus, instead of the proper preparation of a couple of flagons,
as he had specially directed, and as the Princess had
duly commanded; it was the dire conviction of the
ignominious failure in which he was involved, that
made his disgust too deep for words.

He met the Little Lady descending the staircase, but rushed past without a kiss, a word, or a glance.

She knew, only too well, what was before her. At an early hour in the day she had discovered that Contrabandus, so far from being the solution of a problem, was, on the contrary, himself as insoluble a problem as she had ever encountered. He had seated himself comfortably in an easy chair, in the most attractive spot available for his selection, and when she descended to make her daily round of inspection, he was regaling himself with a pipe, and recounting, to an interested group of listeners, gathered from the various departments of household service, temporarily abandoned, his varied perils by field and flood, in the transition from bondage to freedom. The Little Lady dispersed the audience, confiscated the pipe, and ordered Contrabandus up stairs, where, on a subsequent examination, his dense ignorance and absolute barbaric awkwardness were disclosed. Still, she had heard of the aptitude of his race to receive instruction, and of the rapidity with which he was supposed to be rushing into the ranks of intellectual progress, at the call of philanthropy, and she thought she would try her practiced hand upon him in the sphere of duty to which he had been summoned. And this she would do thoroughly, for the Prince's sake, as well as for the good of Contrabandus.

The cloth was thereupon spread and the table set, under the Little Lady's immediate direction, and, in the main, by her own hands; she then seated herself at its head, and in dumb show, and according to the guidance of her voice, and eye, and gesture, caused Contrabandus to perform in her presence. He was not only a willing, but a wildly active scholar, evidently thinking it great fun and engaging in the novel occupation as if it were a new variety of field sport. He plunged to and fro, thrusting before the Princess the empty tureen, distributing plates of imaginary soup, whirling, in mid-air, platters of supposititious fish, make-believe meats, and other fictitious viands, through all the courses of the meal, and making confusion worse confounded with his inevitable and fatal blunders.

In vain did the Princess seek to make him revolve about her in his proper orbit. Twenty times, during this pantomimic rehearsal, was a scene like this enacted. Enter Contrabandus, on full jump, with an empty dish. Princess, with a deprecatory gesture, waves him back. Contrabandus, in the effort to stop, pitches forward. Princess shrieks, menacing him with uplifted forefinger. Contrabandus disappears, and re-enters. Princess encourages him with a beckoning motion of her hand. Contrabandus ducks his head, gathers force for a rapid forward movement, and projects the dish as if bent on bowling down everything on the table. Princess, with open palm, warns him off. Contrabandus misinterprets the gesture as a signal for instant dispatch, and delivers the dish on the middle of the table with a bang which sets everything ringing. Princess, with savage glance, threatens him with annihilation. Exit

Contrabandus, as if his old master were after him, with a shot-gun and a brace of blood-hounds.

The pantomimic dinner bore no comparison in its tragi-comic situations to the real dinner. Some time before it was served, Contrabandus, who had made discovery of a bell, the use of which was strictly prohibited, except in cases of extreme emergency, employed himself in ringing it for an indefinite time—which, to the agonized ears of the Prince and Princess and the startled ears of their guests, seemed much longer than it really was—under the apparent supposition that all the field hands were to be got in. When the company were seated, the Little Lady soon discovered that he had not retained the first faint remembrance of the morning lesson. Whatever instinct served him in stead of memory, had taken him back to the barbecue and the pine grove, and the semi-barbaric antics and revelry of that festal scene.

How the earlier stages of the dinner were accomplished, in the wild disorganization which reigned supreme, under which the well trained, assisting damsel succumbed, in helpless bewilderment, in a corner of the neighboring pantry, and the Princess kept her seat, only because she knew that in every case of a runaway it was safer to sit still than to jump out, neither host, hostess nor guests could afterwards describe. The performances of Contrabandus were like the cyclone, which does its destructive work with a suddenness that so obliterates the consciousness of those whom it buries alive under the crash of universal ruin, that when rescued they cannot tell the tale, either of the shock or of the succor.

The inevitable crisis came at last. Among the oft-repeated injunctions of the Princess, at the morning rehearsal, was one which instructed Contrabandus, at a certain stage of the dinner, and before its final courses, to remove the ample napkin which was invariably spread over the table cloth, in front of the Prince, who was fond of carving, and preferred the ancient order to the more recent fashion, which threatens to make carving a lost art among gentlefolk.

When the point of time was reached at which this mandate should have been executed, the Princess, in a wild effort to bring some trace of order out of chaos, whispered to Contrabandus, as he shot past her, the single word "napkin." He took up, on the instant, a confused recollection of the reiterated command of the morning. The word rang in his ear like the note of a bugle, sounding a charge. The duty of the moment came to him like a sudden inspiration. It was to capture the nearest napkin and remove it out of sight. The guest at the post of honor, at the right hand of the Princess, was at once the object of a strategic movement on his left flank. The snow-white napkin, which lay, in ample folds, across his portly person, in the peaceful discharge of its inanimate, protective duty, was furtively seized by Contrabandus, and snatched away.

Now there is nothing which a well-regulated and

veteran diner-out would be less likely to anticipate, or more likely to resent, than an effort to deprive him, of his napkin, by force, in the middle of a dinner, and at the table of a friend. It is not to be wondered at that the guest at the right hand of the Princess, thus suddenly surprised and attacked, by a natural impulse and by a counter movement, in the nick of time, grasped the rapidly disappearing napkin, at the imminent risk of losing his balance and getting, prematurely, under the table. Contrabandus was checked in full career—but only checked—and the struggle between the combatants became most exciting. Each clinging, with convulsive clutch, to the several ends of the napkin, its broad, snowy band tightly drawn between them, they looked like the famous Siamese Twins, save that what resembled their bond of union, was, in this instance, a sign of discord. Contrabandus, loyal to his mistress, and burning with the zeal of a new convert to free labor, was bent on " havin' dish yer towel, any how," while the victim of his assault, being of heavy weight and somewhat combative in disposition, was disposed to settle the question, at once and forever, of the inalienable rights of a bona-fide napkin holder. It was literally the tug of war. But on which end of the napkin victory would finally have perched, the Muse of History can never sing, for the Prince, at the moment his eye took in the unprecedented situation, with a voice of thunder, demanded unconditional and instant surrender on the part of Contrabandus, who was sum-

marily banished from the banqueting hall in disgrace, to wonder, in his exile, why he should have
been cashiered, on the eve of a brilliant success.

Order having been restored and the rights of
hospitality vindicated, the Prince told his guests the
whole story of Contrabandus, lucifers, Falernian
and all, and the Princess supplemented it by recounting, and, in part, repeating the pantomimic
experiences of the Barmecide feast of the morning,
so that a merrier ending of a meal was hardly ever
known within the palace walls.

The next day, Contrabandus, having made the
timely discovery, "his own self," that the "performances" on the upper side of the invisible line were
"teetotally contrairey to what day is" on the
nether side, was relieved from further indoor duty
and sent off, with well-lined pocket and good
credentials for open air service, to an interior and
strictly rural district, where there are no risks of
illumination; where the juice of the apple, and not
the foaming grape of the Falemian vine is the
favorite beverage; and where napkins are, as yet,
unknown.

6

# CHAPTER X.

IT must, in all candor, be admitted that the Prince was not as wise, or as considerate, in respect to matters in which dealings with Domesticus were concerned, as he was, or was supposed to be, in the management of his own external affairs. He chafed and made himself uncomfortable over many things which the Princess easily schooled herself to endure. What specially exasperated him, and created unceasing irritation, which the lapse of time failed to allay, were the poisoning propensities of Domesticus.

The historic poisoner, the poisoner of the drama and of the romance, worked in secret and did his deadly work by stealth, but the poisons of Domesticus were dispensed in the light of day and greedily consumed by innumerable victims, with their eyes as well as their mouths wide open. He poisoned at the fountain-head. His dealings with the great staple of human sustenance, of which the staff of life is fashioned, by subjecting it to the action of chemical compounds, out of sheer malice, and so contrived as to secure the corrosion of all the stomachs of all the free and enlightened inhabitants of Magna Patria, was, with the Prince, a constant source of wrath and objurgation. It vexed his soul that the prayer for daily bread should be answered in the mixtures of tartaric acid, potassia, and chloride of sodium, which, under various disguises and aliases, had come to be substituted for the leaven of earlier and better days; all in the interest of lie-a-bed and lazy emissaries of Domesticus, who set aside the revered processes of fermentation, and discarded the time-honored yeast-cake, the delight of the old brigade of breadmakers.

The presence, at the morning meal, of a well-heaped pile of products of the oven, hastily compounded with the aid of the last patented preparation with which the evil genius of Chemistry had cursed the finest of the wheat, was like a red rag to a bull. The Prince had an aversion to being poisoned, and he carried it so far as to object to the poisoning of his wife and children. These preparations, he would declare, were poison, slow but sure. All the toothless gums, all the sallow faces, all the spoiled complexions, all the miserable dyspeptics, throughout the length and breadth of Magna Patria, were largely due to this diabolism, of which the cream of Tartarus and the substance held in solution by the Dead Sea were fitting elements and ingredients.

He waged war against the deadly and insidious compounds, in all their forms; he denounced their inventors, manufacturers, and venders, as enemies of

the human race, no matter under cover of how many
copyrights, trade-marks, medals, or medical analyses,
they plied their pernicious arts. Time and again,
he prohibited the use of their wares and forbade
their introduction into the palace, but his interdicts
were all in vain; Domesticus was the sworn ally of
these destroyers, who, while carrying on a perpetual,
internecine war against each other, were leagued, in
common cause, against the entire community, and
so the fatal mixtures, smuggled into every prohibited place, were thrust upon the Prince, in spite of
his teeth, and between his teeth. To no purpose
did he threaten, and proscribe, and issue his search
warrants. He was as powerless as an exciseman
on an Irish coast. The prohibited article could not
be found on any part of the premises, in cup, or can,
or parcel; nobody ever bought it, or brought it, or
saw it, and yet there it was, in inexhaustible supply,
the bane of every breakfast, like the death in the
prophet's pot, with no miraculous healing touch of
Nature at hand, to counteract the malignant evil,
and supply its antidote. So, like Socrates when he
drank the hemlock, the Prince had to convey the
poison to his own lips, not with the serenity of Socrates, but with dire imprecations upon Domesticus,
who, all unseen, laughed in the sleeve in which the
death-drug had been slyly and secretly conveyed
into the palace.

The Princess thought it unreasonable that such
a fuss should be made over what seemed to her a
fixed result in the course of the progress of civil-

ization, which was bringing science to the aid of the
culinary art as well as of all other arts. After all,
she would tell the Prince, when—after unsuspect-
ingly biting through a lump of the saline abom-
ination—he would break out into incipient imprecations, it was a question of skill in the use; gun-
powder and dynamite might be awkwardly handled,
but they were no less valuable means to the ends
for which they were adapted. The Prince would
rejoin, with his teeth on edge, that the people who
were careless in handling these dangerous sub-
stances generally had the evil effects visited summarily, and directly, upon themselves, while the
agents of Domesticus took good care to point their
destructive weapons away from their own persons.

The Prince, finding at last that he was wholly
powerless to carry his point, was forced to content
himself with making every one as uncomfortable as
he could, whenever the presence of the contraband
compounds was detected on the family board. He
talked about the "turnpike" which he insisted was
what his grandmother used for the raising of flour,
and which was something whereof the Little Lady
had never heard, although her education had been
sufficiently thorough for any well conditioned Princess.

She thought it hard that he should expect the
old time and barbarous methods of his ancestors
to be perpetuated in modern palaces, and as for
his fancied "turnpike,"—whatever fermenting or
permeating mixture that may have been,—she did

not believe in its existence, and the word was in no standard dictionary, with a definition justifying his statement. Then the Prince would revert to the scenes of his boyhood, and describe the long array of turnpike cakes, carefully compounded, according to the art and mystery of breadmakers, and being the true leaven, ranged in due order, in the sunniest exposure, to bring into service the direct solar rays in aid of the perfect work they were to accomplish —the transformation of the brayed wheat into the wheaten bread.

The Princess could easily discard these reminiscences, as either too purely fanciful, or too wholly irrelevant in view of their antiquity, and she had too much good sense to attempt to turn back the stream of Time in the interest of any particular method of making biscuits. But while this subject was disposed of without difficulty, there was another, on which the Prince would frequently dilate, which could not be so summarily dismissed. This was the ancestral apple pie. The fondest memories of the Prince for his grandmother seemed to cluster around this pie. He was never tired of talking about it, describing it, and instituting invidious comparisons between it and the spurious article which Domesticus insisted on palming off upon him, in its stead. The genuine grandmother's apple pie differed from the spurious apple pie of Domesticus, in several cardinal points. In the first place, it had apple in it. Secondly, there was no lemon in it. Thirdly, it had no bottom crust. Fourthly, it was not surmounted with any foreign or new-fangled ornamentations, in lieu of the old-fashioned and honest top crust. Fifthly, and lastly, one could eat the whole of it and be never the worse.

Vainly had the Princess striven to have this ideal apple pie reproduced. Domesticus grudged our poor Prince any such souvenir of the Past as a solace for the Present. Apple pie he could have, but only of such sort as to awaken feelings kindred to those of Tantalus, when the swift stream flowed past his lips but just beyond their touch. Domesticus would never give up the bottom crust. He held on to it as if it were a kind of under-lying security for his wages. He would never dispense with the lemon. It was, to him, like the mixture of a lie, which, Lord Bacon says, doth ever please. He clung to the top decoration as tenaciously as an elderly flirt to a false front. As for increasing the quantity of apple, it was an insult to suggest it. Nature made the apple, but he was to make the pie, and his rule was the minimum of apple to the maximum of paste, so that the Little Lady, after many expostulations, entreaties, and commands, and some unsuccessful experimenting, had abandoned the effort to revive for the Prince this lost delight of his youth. She could not silence his regrets nor satisfy his wonderings, why, when everything else that was antique was being revived, the grandmother's apple pie could not be included in the revival; and in her despair, she was tempted to wish that the Prince had never had any grandmother, until she came to reflect, that in such case, there would never have been any Prince.

Besides these instances of maladroitness, the Prince would, sometimes, so far forget himself as to venture untimely allusions to the supposed superior good fortune of other families, in their experience with Domesticus. In such and such a palace of a friendly prince there might be found the accredited representatives of Domesticus, who had remained under the roof for two or three consecutive decades; who were happy and who diffused happiness. There, the same familiar faces which had greeted the Prince in his younger days, at the open portal, still yielded him the accustomed welcome, now that his visits were rarer, and a new generation had intervened. Or, he would describe how at some repast served upon an antique table, with carved, claw-footed legs, spread with heir-looms in glass, and china, and silver, there would hover about the board some old ministering genius, dark and polished as the table-top itself, and held in high esteem as a relic of the ancient days to which all these souvenirs belonged.

How these better fortunes came to their possessors the Princess could not divine, but she was unable to rid herself of a feeling that their contemplation was a source of unavailing regret to the Prince. It seemed, to her sensitive nature, a kind of treason against the sovereignty of home, a sacrilege against the household gods, for a pater-familias to acknowledge that anything, under a stranger's roof-tree, was superior to what he could find under his own. If he were forced to the consciousness of inferiority and tempted to its avowal, it was a condemnation of the incapacity which permitted it, and which must be repented of in sack-cloth and ashes.

The efforts of the Prince to disabuse her mind of these wrong impressions were not apt to be successful. He was himself, not infrequently, in a state of exasperation against Domesticus, induced not only by his special devices, but by his general and continuous violation of all the laws of trade.

To pay the highest price for the best service, to give the most for skilled labor, was right and well enough, but to pay these prices and to get, in return, the poorest service, and the densest ignorance, was to be made the victim of intolerable imposition. When the carefully selected joint appeared before the Prince, in a state of readiness for the plate and the palate, only a little advanced beyond that in which it had been sold in the shambles, and a whole company must needs wait, with unappeased appetite, until it had been gashed into bits and sent below stairs, to undergo a supplementary culinary process, to fit it for mastication, there were no limits to the punishments he would devise against the perpetrator of such a crime. It was fraud and falsehood for any one to make pretensions which resulted in such flagrant failure. It involved deliberate deception and dishonesty, because it was proof positive that all the declarations and representations of capacity were false. In any other department of dealings, between man and man, such crimes would send the criminal to the penitentiary and the State-prison; but in the case of Domesticus he must be paid and pampered while he went on, spoiling the supplies, abusing the property, and destroying the digestion and the temper of his employer. It was not a matter, the Prince would say, of fifteen pounds of beef, ruined by being sent up half raw, or another fifteen pounds, equally ruined, by being cooked to a crisp. It was a matter of principle. It struck at the foundations of Society. It concerned the great law of supply and demand, and of the relations between capital and labor, and if Domesticus were to be exempt from all obligations—legal, social, and moral—communism and nihilism, and every other baneful, destructive, and accursed ism, abroad in a wicked world, would be let loose, and universal anarchy was only a question of time.

The Princess, who was selfish enough to be less immediately concerned about the foundations of society than about the harmony of her household, and the happiness of her Prince, was too ready to take all these vehement tirades as, in some sense, a reflection upon her internal administration.

Then the Prince would emphatically declare that it was not the Little Lady who was in fault, nor her co-sufferers and fellow victims. He would insist that the fact that nothing had happened to her which did not come to all of her sex and station, was proof of his contention, and that the exceptional cases of success or exemption, which he sometimes cited, only served to make good the general rule. But she invariably found that the sole result of these periodical outbursts was to put upon her the burden and responsibility of a summary dismissal of the delinquents who excited them, and the procurement and substitution of their successors.

It would have been well for the Prince if he had confined himself to occasional denunciations of Domesticus, but, in spite of the repeated warnings he had received, in his failures already recounted, he would persist in forcing upon the Princess suggestions which were wholly impracticable, and which, instead of alleviating her distresses, only aggravated them. One of these, and, perhaps, the most ill advised and unpalatable, was the periodical proposition of a housekeeper. The Princess Otiosa had a housekeeper and everything went on like clock-work, in her palace. In the great ancestral realm of Mater Patria the housekeeper was a permanent institution. Domesticus himself was subject, and had been, from time immemorial, to her delegated authority. There, the flowerets of the family were potted and trained in the plantarium for such tender shoots, tended by the nursery governess, and the general routine of the household was in the hands of the housekeeper, so that the mistress of the mansion was not tied down to the details and drudgery which beset her here. Why not copy the good ways of the mother country?

Such suggestions as these would bring every

drop of maternal and patriotic blood in the veins of the Little Lady to the boiling point. She would have none of the ways of Mater Patria. If she could not rule her own house, she did not want a roof to her head. A housekeeper, forsooth—as if, with all her cares, and anxieties, and toils, this new and greater burden were to be imposed on her, and she to be set aside, as unfit to manage her own palace, and be put on the retired list, and told to twirl her thumbs and do nothing !

And to tear the dear children from her, and put sticks in the plantarium for the little tendrils of their hearts to twine about, instead of the maternal stock, with its native roots and its encircling branches! It was all well enough in Mater Patria, where everything ran in grooves, cut centuries ago, which it was a part of national pride and duty to keep, forever, at the same depth, and width, and distance, and divergence. Over there, housekeepers and nursery governesses might fill places in the household, as permanent as maids of honor in the royal court. But not here, where every right-minded woman wants to know what is going on in her house, and not be kept in the dark by intermediates between her, and her children, and her servants. And as for the Princess Otiosa, what could the Prince, or any other man, know about the real state of the case? Had she not, herself, admitted, at countless afternoon teas and in all social circles, that her housekeeper was a nuisance, and was not the Princess Blandiloqua fairly driven out of her palace

by the nursery governess, who came between her
and her husband, and how could any well-regulated
prince look his princess in the face and propose such
subversive and humiliating changes ?

The Prince was always glad to beat a retreat from
this particular line, although never wise enough to
abstain entirely, as he ought to have done, from excursions into the dangerous sphere of discussion
into which the doings of Domesticus invited. In
fact, it was, sometimes, impossible to avoid being
insensibly drawn thither, as into an ambuscade,
because of the innumerable occasions in which the
last trial to which the Princess had been subjected,
or the latest disturbance of his own peace and comfort, or the recital of new enormities practiced on
some relative or friend, was the topic of the hour.
From the particular instance, the Prince would, naturally, diverge to the general subject, and presently
would become entangled in the whole vast, intricate,
and inextricable theme of Domesticus. The Prince
had a large stock of unsettled views on this topic,
but as they had never been subjected to any practical test, the Princess gradually found that they
were valuable only in theory, and that Domesticus
was a problem she must solve by herself.

And she was nearer its solution than she knew.
She had, during the long years of her probation,
from which we have drawn only a few scattered
incidents, been bringing to the study of Domesticus, in all his ways and in every department of

his shiftless doings, the kind of minute scrutiny and microscopic observation which Darwin gave to the manœuvres and mound building of those real workers, the ants in his garden; and she had come to know and understand the subject of her study, just as the great naturalist knew the omni-meandering and ravaging insects, in all their devious ins and outs. Compared with her certain knowledge of facts and her accumulated store of experience, of what value were the speculations of the Prince?

The Little Lady could not reason, or draw deductions, or construct a syllogism, but she knew all that any one could know about Domesticus, and for her to hear the Prince discourse on this subject was as if an old mariner, who had sailed all the seas, without ever being taught the science of navigation, were to be instructed in seamanship by a college sophomore or a student of theology. What she wanted was not dissertations on the relation between employer and the employed, or on the supposed short comings of mistresses as the cause whereof the delinquencies of maids were the effect, but sympathy, and forbearance, and a tender sense of the hard conditions by which the symmetry of her home life, so precious in her sight, and so sacredly guarded by her care, was, in spite of all her efforts, being constantly chipped, at its delicate edge, by the rasping contact with Domesticus. She gave less and less heed to the generalizations of the Prince, and as these sounded, more and more, like empty verbiage, so did his particular instances of better conditions elsewhere, real or imaginary, become less and less disturbing.

All unconsciously, she was coming towards the possession, in her own right, of whatever clue there may be in this tangled labyrinth. It was with her as it is with so many of her sex. The road to truth did not lie over the great causeways and viaducts of reason, constructed by skilled hands and by scientific methods, but by a native right of way, through instinct, sensibility, and the heart. Thus helped, when seemingly most helpless, she had, like a pioneer in the unexplored forest, blazed her own path in the wilderness thickets into which Domesticus had driven her, and she was beginning to know her way. In the treacherous pitfalls, she was planting some sure stepping-stones. She could not explain to others, or formulate for herself, the results she had attained, or even fully trust the strength they gave, but she knew she was stronger, and she believed she was going towards the light.

The strong foundation of her quiet confidence, although she knew it not, was her abiding, native sense of justice. This is the true rock on which all human relations must subsist. It is like the great stones on which the Temple stood. She had come to feel, rather than to know how largely this great primal law was set at nought in the dealings of Domesticus, who himself knew no law, and taught his followers none, save the law of self defence and the law of retaliation.

Now what we call justice is, in human affairs, simply, generosity in its highest action. Were the true, generic stamp of human nature undefaced, no native, and because native, no generous act would ever meet a base return, but only its just equivalent, in reciprocal acts of kindliness and service, and justice would be the all-pervading rule of life. In spite of our degeneracy, which turns justice into a lawgiver and an avenger, and which puts and keeps the race, of necessity, under her behest, or her ban, there are some fine natures, in which the love of justice, for its own sake, shines in something of its original brightness, set in crystalline beauty, in the central adamant of the soul. Our Little Lady was the unconscious possessor of this rare treasure, and it was the talisman whose use and power she was, by degrees and only imperfectly, learning.

Her knowledge came only by long discipline. She had found that to understand and to rule Domesticus, she must, herself, be capable of doing his work. Only thus could she stand on a vantage ground of absolute justice in her dealings with him. To exact honesty and integrity in the doing of his work, and success in its results, might be impossible, but a great step toward these ends was gained when she showed the shirking, or recreant non-worker that the thing she required could not only be done well, and according to her standard, but that she could do it herself. Not only had her fair, jewelled finger been pointed to every nook and cor-

ner, from which the scouring sand or the cleansing
brush **had** been wickedly or surreptitiously withheld,
**or** from which the uplifted duster had been furtively
withdrawn; she had herself dragged, from **long-
closed** cupboards and from tuck-holes—abominated
by the true housewife—their slatternly **accumula-
tions.** She would **go on her** knees, if occasion **re-**
quired, for the instant completeness of the work, as
readily upon **a** hearth stone **or the** hall floor, as
upon a hassock in the **proudest shrine.**

**Many** things which **Domesticus pretended to do
and was** paid for doing, and never **did, she not only
did, with** unerring skill, **but taught the way of doing,
though well** knowing **it was labor perhaps lost so
far as her own** personal **advantage was concerned.**
The fine yellow meal of **Magna Patria, its** best gold-
dust, she could coin into rare products **most** satisfying **to sense** and taste, while in the heavy, untrained
**hand of Domesticus it** was invariably spoiled, and
**wasted, and condemned, as better** fitted for the hen-
coop than **the breakfast** table. **She** could turn aside
from the **tender ministries of the sick room, to take
into** her **own fair hand the viand with which she**
hoped **to tempt the** appetite **of the** convalescent, **or**
the invalid, **hold it,** with dextrous manipulation, **over
the** glowing **coals** of the quick fire, lighted **under
her** own eye, **for the** exact time required **to bring it
to** perfection, and then serve **it,** herself, at the instant,
**so** that its flavor seemed a **new** revelation to its recipient.

**Like the Roman** conquerors, **she** learned from

7

her enemies.    Wherever a device or a method, known, or half known, to Domesticus, had in it the possibility of improvement, she made it subservient to her skill and her quick sense of observation, until, little by little, without descending from her proper sphere, she knew and was certain, that in every department of the daily service she could, if it were necessary, herself surpass her servitors.    And yet there were some things which seemed impossible and beyond her reach, and one of these was the grandmother's apple-pie.    But even of this she did not despair, for hope was of the essence of her sunlit soul.

# CHAPTER XI.

THE Imperial City was full of seekers after Fortune. Like the Virgins in the Scriptures, some of them were wise and some of them were foolish. Among the wise, few were wiser than Juventus. From the Northern forest-clearing whence he came, from the rushing, never-failing streams, into whose depths he had cast his line, long before he threw it into the troubled metropolitan waters, from the bleak rock-ribbed uplands where he had braved the winter winds, before he came to buffet with the storms of fate, he brought with him, as his whole patrimony, three priceless gifts,—strength, courage, and poverty.

The sages of his tribe, after their simple fashion, had taught him out of their wisdom which came from close contact, day and night, winter and summer, with the earth and the air. Like the sorcerers who could tame wild horses with whispered words and charm away witches with rosemary, they had their own secret spells by which Nature was made subservient to the human will. They never wandered out of sight of the smoke wreaths of their cabins, but their touch could turn the tall, forest

99

pine into the shapely mast and send it forth, no
longer to sigh and murmur in the midnight wind,
but, bending under the weight of outspread sails,
to rise, and dip, and plunge, through calm and storm,
from ocean to ocean, till its path had girdled the
globe.   They sent Juventus forth, to make his own
way, where all ways met.   They bade him be brave
and wary, staunch of will and strong of purpose;
to add to his courage, constancy, and to constancy,
vigilance, and to vigilance, untiring toil.

As the Roman youths found their way to Athens,
he went to sit at the feet of the philosophers in the
schools, where he was taught in the wisdom of the
ancients and the moderns, and where, by dint of
some native genius and much severe discipline, he
came to see his name written with honor on the
Academic roll, and to become foremost as an athlete
on the Campus, as well as in the contests for scho-
lastic prizes.

Thus equipped, Juventus was cast into the whirl-
pool of the Imperial City, to swim for himself.  He
was a stranger among strangers, facing his unknown
future, with a bright open countenance, a modest
resoluteness, and an honest readiness to do, with his
might, whatsoever his hand found to do.   He
knocked at many doors, to find them shut and
barred, until it seemed as if there were no vacant
space, or chink, or crevice, in all the world of
working forces by which he was at once encom-
passed and excluded.

He consulted the oracles.

At first their responses seemed to him dubious and discouraging, but, after long waiting and much pondering, he began to discern the possible meaning of their utterances, and at last, in his own experience, he found the best interpretation.

To his question, " Where is the way to success?" the answer—" Find the royal road and it will lead thither,"—seemed to him to contradict what he had always been taught, that there was no such royal road. Later, he learned that for every sovereign will, crowned with a true purpose, there is a king's highway thrown up, which surely leads, if not to the loftiest summits of success, to its high vantage grounds.

To his question, " When shall I succeed?" the answer—" When good luck comes,"—seemed to him strangely at variance with the oft-repeated saying that luck is the refuge of fools. But, by and by, he came to comprehend that good luck means only opportunity, waited for, watched for, seized at sight, and held with firm grasp.

To his question, " What is the secret of success?" the answer, in a single word,—" Dependence,"— seemed a poor substitute, almost a mockery, for the braver sound " Independence," which he had waited to hear. But, after a while, he was schooled to discern the truth that his is the highest success who, in service, in rule, or in heroic action, exhibits not so much his own independence of his fellows, as their constant need of him and their dependence upon him. To be the earliest to take up the daily task, however humble ; the last to quit the post of duty, however obscure ; to be the quickest of eye, the readiest of hand, the fleetest of foot ; the most sagacious to perceive, the most skillful to plan, the most diligent to execute ; the most faithful in trust and the most fearless for the right, means, for every such servitor, in whatever sphere, final mastery and supremacy. He is the most successful of all men who can best bear the heaviest weight of human interests, and so best serve his kind.

Juventus, fortunately, had learned how to be patient and how to wait. His special study and training had been in the all-embracing science which, from its rudimental stage of star-gazing, has come to deal with whatsoever things can be measured, or numbered, or computed, or set in relation to other things and to the universe, and which, being the foundation of all most effective mechanical skill, as well as of all high processes of reasoning, had furnished him for the best service of hand and brain, and given him a training which helped him to wait without idleness, and to hope without impatience.

At last, he succeeded, after many fruitless attempts, and as many disappointments, in finding his way into the inner workshop of a wizard, renowned for his dealing with hidden forces and his marvelous inventive skill in bringing them, by curious appliances, contrived and wrought out of his special arcana, into the daily service of mortals. More skillful than Boethius, who is said to have made

singing birds out of brass, he could, as he showed
at a later stage of his inventions, bring the articu-
lations of human speech out of inanimate materials, and even at this earlier period he was giving
rare indications of his weird control over invisible
elements and powers.

He was busied, when Juventus entered, working
with his own hands, and absorbed in an experiment,
having for its object the ascertainment of the exact
relative proportions in which certain liquids should
be mixed in water to produce a chemical compound,
the properties of which he wished to avail of in the
operation of one of his machines. To this end he
was patiently filling vessels of varying size and
capacity, and pouring from one to another, with
steady hand and keenly observant eye. He did not
pause an instant on the entrance of Juventus, but,
by his manner, seemed to permit his presence as no
intrusion or disturbance, recognizing in the new
comer, from the account given him by the friend
who had secured his admission, a novice in the
occult arts in which he was, himself, so renowned a
master. But as his mastery was by self-taught
methods which ignored, and held somewhat in
disdain, the teachings of the schools, he looked
without special interest on this scion of the Acad-
emy.

Juventus stood, for some time, a silent and interested observer of the wizard's work. Presently,
when it seemed as if another hand might, opportunely, aid its progress, he quietly stepped forward

and gave his help, so deftly, and with such intelligent appreciation of the character of the experiment, that his service was accepted, without rebuff, and presently, the two men were working together, in dead silence and dead earnest, until, at length, the slow process of measuring the liquids and of arriving at the desired result was successfully concluded.

Then Juventus, who had by this time grasped the whole scope of the inventor's experiment, which was a matter of simple chemistry, took from the rude table in the work-room a scrap of paper, and by a rapid marshalling of figures and signs, and a brief calculation, reached and set in plain terms, amounting to absolute demonstration, the same result as to the required relative proportions of the chemicals which had made necessary for its ascertainment, by actual manipulation and measurement, the labor of hours. He modestly placed the paper before the wizard, who looked at the figures and nodded assent at the result, but shook his head, scornfully, at the process by which it was reached.

"My way is best for me, because it is my own, and your calculation only proves that I was right, of which I needed no proof. Book-men are apt to become mere machines themselves, instead of machine makers. I will have none of their ways. But there may be work for you in the outer shop, and I see you know how to use hand as well as head. You can try," and, opening the door leading into the loft which served as a shop, and shoving Juventus forth, he made a sign and whispered a word to a workman in charge, the result of which was that a day's mechanical work for a day's wages was offered, and was forthwith availed of, by our fortune seeker.

The thing which Juventus was set to do was the putting together of the related parts of a new and delicate instrument, a pet offspring of the wizard's inventive brain, by which men were to be enabled to multiply the transmission of messages over great distances, magically conveyed, by methods whereof he knew the charm and secret. Juventus willingly applied himself to this humble task, and resumed it on the next day, having been duly enrolled on the staff of workmen in the factory. During the morning, after putting together and adjusting with precision and accuracy the separate and delicate parts of the mechanism to his own satisfaction, it happened that at the moment of completion, he was told to take it into the inner work-shop, where the wizard had just called for a finished instrument. Placing it on the table, and receiving a nod of recognition from the wizard, Juventus said :

"May I venture a word about this piece of work ? "

"Say on," said the wizard.

"Here," said Juventus, placing his finger upon the instrument, "is a superfluous screw. It can easily be dispensed with. Bring these two an eighth of an inch nearer each other and—"

"You are right, entirely right," said the wizard,

interrupting him, his quick gesture showing that his eye took in the whole suggested change, at once, and that no further word was needed. " That will save a day's work on every instrument. When you come to-morrow, do not stay out yonder. I want you here."

And so good luck came to Juventus.

# CHAPTER XII.

## A GRANDMOTHER'S APPLE-PIE.

ONE bright morning the Prince was about leaving his palace for his daily round of duty, when, as he kissed the Little Lady, with accustomed tenderness, he asked her, as was also his wont, what he should send home?

"We had chops and sweet-breads yesterday," she murmured, returning his embrace.

This statement, as a reminiscence, might be supposed to have some possible interest, but, as it threw no light on the subject of his inquiry, the Prince persevered.

"What shall it be, dearest, I am in something of a hurry."

"O dear," said the Princess, "why cannot we live without eating? Send anything you please, there is nothing now, except beef, and mutton, and poultry."

"A piece of beef to roast?" said the Prince. This was an original suggestion which he was in the habit of making, almost every morning, under the same circumstances.

"No," said the Princess, "you will want that to-morrow."

"Chickens?" said the Prince.

"Oh, she spoils poultry."

"She spoils everything," said the Prince, getting a little out of patience.

"Well, what am I to do? She is the tenth since Christmas, and they are all alike."

"Break up housekeeping," said the Prince, in a determined tone of voice, "rent the palace, and go to the Via Quinta Hotel."

"What, take these dear, precious children to a place where they would never have a morsel of plain, wholesome food, and have to associate with people you know nothing about, and deprive them of a home; I would starve first!"

And the Princess sat down on the nearest settle, in a way that made the Prince tremble.

"Of course," said he, "home is better for the children, and for all of us—only I am afraid Domesticus is going to be the death of you."

"Perhaps he will be," said the Princess, dismally, giving way, for the moment, to foreboding, "and if I could only be sure that my darling children would be properly cared for, I should die happy, but the thought of a step-mother—"

"Oh, don't speak to me so," cried the Prince, frightened out of his wits, and as he clasped the Princess in his arms, and she gradually grew reconciled to the prospect of continued life, she whispered in his ear—he looking furtively at his watch, meanwhile—

"I suppose it had better be porter-house steaks."

**And** porter-house steaks **it was.**

Hardly had the great door closed on **her departing** spouse, before the Little Lady became thoroughly ashamed of the momentary weakness to **which she** had given **way.** She knew very well, that however feebler vessels of **her** sex might succumb, and **fly** to foreign parts, or to hotels, **or** lodgings, **she** had no more intention **or** fear of being done **to** death by Domesticus, than she had of being divorced from her husband. **She knew** she was getting **the better of Domesticus every day and that his com-** plete **conquest was only a question of time.** She betook **herself to her arm chair, and as she curled** herself in **its** encircling **and comforting embrace,** regretted, more and more, **that she had shown the** white feather, even for **a** moment; yet she excused herself, partly, as she might well have done wholly, in the retrospect of some sharp trials, recent and **remote,** which had jarred **her** nerves, and tried her **temper, and left her almost at** her wits' end, **all unknown to the Prince, or to any one else.**

**Then she revolved in her mind many things which** brought to **her, gradually, a sense of relief and sat-** isfaction. **She was** no longer **in the dark, or in** doubt, **about Domesticus.** She saw clearly, **and** knew thoroughly, **all** that was needed **to be seen or** known, and she **could be** just to **him** and **to her-** self. After charging **to his** long, dark, unsettled account, all his sins **of omission and** commission, **all his** high crimes and misdemeanors, as well **as** his inferior and innumerable pecadilloes, **was he,**

after all, as black as he was painted, or as she had
often pictured him during her long, bitter warfare?
Could she not give Domesticus his due, while exacting to the uttermost, what was due from him to
herself? If ignorance was inwrought in every fibre
of his constitution, was not ignorance the normal
state of every untaught being? If idleness was
the breath of his nostrils, was it not the natural
corrosive of all human energy, uninspired and un-
impelled by adequate motive? If ingratitude was
his constant requital for kindness, was not this base
alloy common to all unrefined natures? If insub-
ordination was his besetting sin, was it not the
primal vice of the whole brotherhood of man?
After all, if the many nations of the earth are of
one blood, were they not all marred by the same
blow? Of what avail the charity that suffereth
long, if it cannot suffer the manners and the want
of manners, the short comings and the long wanderings of Domesticus, and learn to put up patiently
with him, as with so many other evils, real or fancied?

The Little Lady, as she pursued her mental retrospect, in this spirit, found herself readily conced-
ing, that with the exception of the dishonesty of
the thieving Hebe, the pang of which no time could
efface, and of occasional invasions of the minor
rights of property, less criminal than careless, the
whole uninventoried possessions of the Prince and
herself, and of her children and guests, in all the
height and length and breadth of the palace, had

been safe, through many revolving years, in the care and custody of Domesticus. And how much real service had been the result of his daily and nightly toil, even when over-rewarded, or grudgingly rendered, or only in part performed, and with a blundering hand? Judged by the test and measure of temptation resisted, and evil example and influence withstood, was not virtue, pre-eminently, the rule with his many emissaries, and vice the exception? Taken as a class, she asked herself, where, in all the history of communities, could be found a fairer record of unstained character than among the myriad workers, of the weaker sex, in the households, high and low, of the Imperial City?

These things, and many other things, the Little Lady meditated, as she sat in her great easy chair, with her invisible thinking-cap on her head, her hands folded, her eyes half shut, and her face, not clouded, but only shadowed, with grave thoughts which followed one another in quick succession, as light clouds drift athwart the summer sky. She had learned so much and gained so much by her long experience, that the self-confidence and resolution she now felt established within her, she knew were genuine, her own possessions, not borrowed or picked up, or won by chance, but gained by her own unaided toil and skill, and therefore hers by absolute right. And to these elements was added the ability to use them, so that, by degrees, she came to the clear comprehension of the truth that real mastery is not by plans or contrivances, however ingenious, for making over the world, but by simply acting so as to make the most and the best of it as it is.

"That which is crooked cannot be made straight," said the Little Lady to herself, "and if Domesticus, like so many other things, and so many other persons, is irretrievably crooked, why should I wonder that he does not make himself straight, and become, all at once—what everybody is blaming him for not being—absolutely perfect."

At the end of her meditations, being now in a glow and fervor of self-reliance, beyond any she had ever felt before, the Princess rose and girded herself with a clean and wide linen apron, and laid aside all her rings, save only her wedding ring, and said further to herself, "I must do penance for my fault of this morning. I will try once more to make a grandmother's apple-pie and this time I mean to succeed."

This high resolve was put into immediate execution.

She was greatly aided in its accomplishment by a timely gift, made to the Prince, by a friend, in a rural district, of a barrel of the required fruit of the sole description worthy, in the estimation of the Prince, of being devoted to so high a use. Of all the varied products with which Pomona, goddess of fruits, enriches the soil of Magna Patria, none so full of virtue as that type of rounded perfectness which gives its name to the very centre of the organ by which the soul looks out on Nature. Of all the many varieties of this first of fruits, the Prince maintained that none could compare—for all the purposes of the culinary art—with one choice kind which, in his boyhood, he had gathered in the upland, ancestral orchard, the apple of the pointed hill top, the Spitzenberg, as men named it in the market place, whose deep red, delicate skin enfolded a spicy flavor unrivalled and unapproachable, if only the dexterous, initiated hand could draw it forth.

The Prince had never read the Epigrams of Martial, but, without knowing that he borrowed from that illustrious author, he had frequently, in his own modern phrase, expressed the sentiment which declares that "Art is not enough for a cook; he must have the taste of his master." But, alas! that taste Domesticus would never acquire, nor could it be imparted to an unwilling recipient, and to have a barrel of Spitzenbergs in his cellarium, with no one capable of extracting their hidden flavor and transferring it to the palate, was rather an aggravation than a solace.

The Princess entered the arena where her self-imposed ordeal was to be endured, with a light, firm step and a beaming face. The time had been when crossing its threshold, on such an errand, she would have encountered fierce frowns and arms a-kimbo, and a discordant clanging of pans and pots, culminating in a pitched battle with Domesticus. But now that she knew all the wiles and stratagems of the enemy, she was able to condense the history of a campaign such as that upon which she was now

8

entering, into as brief a compass as Cæsar's famous
bulletin. She came, saw, and conquered. What
she saw, was a display of pent up wrath which she
knew very well was stirred to its lowest depths by
this sudden invasion, and would doubtless make
the price of success, should she succeed, as great a
penalty as could be inflicted, and yet it dared not
break out in open revolt against the invincible air
and aspect of the Princess, in whose little hand the
rolling pin was as complete a symbol of sovereignty
as was the sceptre of Charlemange in his iron
grasp.

And now, wonderful to relate, but as true as the
most trivial incident recorded in this narrative, as
the Little Lady began her task, and, gradually, the
various ingredients which she required for its performance were set in order, and measured, and mingled, by her own dainty fingers, all unseen to her,
and invisible to mortal eye, came trooping back, not
the entire body, but a select and picked detachment
of the same good fairies who had decamped, years
before, when she began the combat with Domesticus, single handed and alone. This returning pha-
lanx were ever on the alert, a hovering and recon-
noitering force, swift to espy where true courage in
the feeblest mortal entered the lists against destructive powers of the air, and ready to fly to their succor. Only they could not interfere against Domesticus, in behalf of any struggling victims of his
machinations who had not by their unaided efforts
earned the right to such invisible and sure support.

According to the wisdom of the ancients, who declared that the divinities helped those who helped themselves, so did the good fairies of this time leave to the wicked arts and treacherous devices of Domesticus all the many subjects of his power who were not of such stuff as to persevere, until they discovered the secret of deliverance, in learning to do for themselves all the things he pretended to do for them.

This secret the Little Lady had learned and knew she had learned, and now that she came to test her strength to the uttermost, all unaided as it seemed, these unseen, nimble adjutants were on the alert, to bring her aid and comfort, and be her invisible allies. They perched on the edges of the amphora in which the materials of the projected pie were enclosed. They steadied the eye, and guided the hand of the Little Lady, as the work went on. They nerved her to reject, with calm disdain, the proffer of lemon, wherewith Domesticus tempted her, in the critical moment. They strengthened her to persist, against threatenings of disaster and ruin, in placing the gleaming segments of the Spitzenbergs on the shining glazed bottom of the deep dish, without deposit of any intervening substance. Finally, they hovered round the oven door and kept watch and ward over the fortunes of the completed pie, which, as a last resort, Domesticus would fain have ruined in the baking, by a malicious intermeddling with dampers, had not the agile sprites, by swift discharges of their invisible artillery—to human sight, only chance scintillations of red-hot sparks—warded off the traitorous attack, and ensured the triumphant success of this labor of love.

The victory being fully achieved, the Little Lady sought an interval of repose in her own apartment. This was suddenly broken in upon, by the tidings that Decima, of whom dishonorable mention had been made by the Princess in the morning, as the "tenth since Christmas," was about to depart from the palace, in high dudgeon, and was demanding her wages.

"Send Decima to me," said the Princess, wholly unconcerned, and with a sense of relief at parting with number ten which fully compensated for any concern as to the coming of number eleven.

"What is the matter?" she asked, when the self-exiled Decima, enveloped in full outgoing attire, and with a very inflamed visage, appeared on the door-sill. "Are you going away, because I chose to make an apple-pie in my own house?"

Decima had prepared a valedictory which was quite perfect, to her thinking, but which, slightly marred in the delivery, ran, somewhat, on this wise:

"Its me with seventeen years experience that never was insulted before by a lady and if it was leaving out lemons was wanted which every genteel respectable family knows that lemons is needed in apple-pies and indeed where would the apple be but for the lemon unless it is plain pastry for taverns and such likes and if it is the bottom crust was to be saved and skimping the likes of that I never saw

and no lady would begrudge it and to see it before
me own eyes which has lived with the first families
and it is me character which is as good as any ones
and its all the same as being turned away without
warning and its me full month's wages I'm wanting."

"When did you come, Decima?" said the Princess, who, during this harangue, had been going
through a somewhat bewildering mental calculation,
in an effort to divide twenty-five sestertia by eighteen
and had become inextricably entangled in the vulgar fraction which confronted her.

"Day after to-morrow three weeks and me month
is up on the sixteenth it is," said Decima, by way of
adding greater obscurity to the calculation.

"You came at night and you are going away, of
your own accord, before dinner, so that you are
really entitled to only eighteen days wages at the
rate of twenty-five sestertia for the month, but I will
call it nineteen days or say twenty, so as to make it
two-thirds of a month,"—this was a concession in
the interest of the vulgar fraction, as the Princess
saw that to divide twenty-five by nineteen was even
more hopeless than the attempt to divide it by
eighteen, and she caught at a round number, as a
short way out of her difficulty.

But she was not yet clear of her fraction, for now
she must divide twenty-five by twenty, and she had
to pause for a further computation.

"Well, Decima, I will pay you seventeen sestertia,
which is more, a great deal more, than is due you.
If your wages were twenty-four sertertia, two-thirds

would be sixteen," said the Little Lady, continuing
her calculation aloud, "and two-thirds of one sestertium—to make twenty-five, would be—well, seventy-
five is near enough, and I will call it a sestertium,
so here is the money, and I am sorry you are so
foolish."

Decima had not pursued the mental, or oral arith-
metic of her mistress. A month's wages, to her,
meant twenty-five sestertia—no more, nor less—and
for this amount in its integrity, she had come to
make a stand, but there was that in the gesture of
the Princess, as she placed the money in the
woman's hand, which showed, plainly, that not a
sestertium or its smallest part, beyond the proffered
sum, was to be gained, by threat or entreaty. She
was as thoroughly mistress of her money, as of her
mansion.

"And it's not me month's wages I am to get and
ye a rich lady and it's the likes of ye that rob poor
girls and a shame it will be to ye as long as ye live
and its a bad name I'll give ye—it is—and I will,"
and with these mutterings Decima closed her red
fingers on the sestertia, turned her back, and was
seen no more, in the palace of the Princess.

The Prince came home in great spirits. He
rarely brought the topics of his principality into the
domain of home, but before dinner, on this somewhat eventful day, he told the Princess that he had
been playing the grab game, quite successfully.
This was something at which the Dry Goods Princes

were very expert when occasion required. In this particular instance, as the Prince explained, a certain unconscionable scoundrel, from a distant part of Magna Patria, had contrived, under the guise of innocent purchases from the Prince, at short credit, to get into his wicked possession a large quantity of staple commodities, without the slightest intention of ever paying for them. This was plainly shown by his nefarious conduct when he got them to his far-off home, where he was a large and prosperous dealer, as was supposed, but where he suddenly shut his doors and turned over, to a confederate, all the property in his possession. Thereupon, the Prince had betaken himself to his jurisconsults, Meum, Tuum & Suum, who were learned in all the laws of Magna Patria, and knew the Pandects, Edicts and Digests by heart, and who, in their learning and wisdom, sent forth a pursuer, swift as Mercury, quite as unscrupulous, and twice as shrewd, who pounced upon the defrauding dealer and his whole stock in trade, with a mandate, or precept, known, in that part of Magna Patria where the goods were found, as an attachment. This powerful mandate was placed in the hands of a lictor, who in speedy course of justice, by breaking open doors, and seizing property, and making sales, and otherwise exerting the machinery of the law, had secured and got the Prince's whole debt, in money, with interest and costs, and lictor's fees and poundage.

This last word seemed so tremendous, as the

Prince gave it forth, by way of climax, that the Little Lady, in the tenderness of her heart, could not help saying, she hoped they did not pound the poor fellow too hard, even if he was so great a scamp.

Then the Prince laughed, and explained to her that poundage did not mean pounding, at all, but meant the lictor's fees, in addition to his other fees.

"But why is it called poundage?" asked the Princess; "it seems a very queer name for fees."

"I suppose," said the Prince, who, having recovered his debt, was ready to take almost any risk in connection with this venture, "it is because when people get into the lictor's hands, they are like cattle in a pound, and cannot be got out without paying."

This definition was thoroughly satisfactory to the Princess, and then, to show her interest in the story, and her sympathy with the Prince, in his success, she inquired if he found his own goods on the premises of the rogue.

"Yes," said the Prince; then the Princess asked why he did not take them back, instead of selling the other creditors' goods and collecting the money.

The Prince seemed, for some reason, to think this was a capital joke and so expressed himself, and laughed again, very heartily, and the Princess laughed too, to keep him company, although she could not see the joke.

They sat down to dinner, and in due course, the apple-pie made its appearance, and was set before the Prince. Surely no one will grudge a moment's delay for a description of this historic pie. It was embedded in a deep, round, yellowish dish, the top crust swelling slightly from the rim, tinged at every point of its periphery with the exuding juice of the apple, its top embrowned—not scorched—with a warmer wave of the oven heat, while, underneath the flaky tissues of the outer covering, layer on layer, like the leaves of a full-blown rose, overlapping and crowding each other, yet each individual and distinct, lay the amber-colored segments of the Spitzenbergs, clear and translucent, with no perfidious bottom crust to absorb their generous juices or spoil their natural flavor.

When the pie was opened, the Prince began to say:—

" Did Decima make this pie?"

" Decima has gone," said the Princess.

"A good riddance," said the Prince, as he helped the Princess to the first piece of pie. " I knew she never made it."

" I declare," said the Prince, as he placed a portion on the plate for Prima, there is apple in this pie, which, for an apple-pie, is a most extraordinary thing."

Then, as he put his spoon down into its depths, like a mariner sounding in an unknown sea, and struck the smooth surface underneath, "Upon my word," said the Prince, "there is no bottom crust to this pie," and he helped Secundus and Tertia, respectively, to liberal shares.

The Prince then provided, in due course, for himself, and after the first taste, he laid down his knife and fork, looked at the Princess, and exclaimed :—

"Wonders will never cease! There is no lemon in this pie!"

"Of course not," said the Princess.

"And the flavor is not all cooked out of the apples," cried the Prince. "They have the real, genuine, Spitzenberg taste."

"Certainly they have," said the Princess.

" I verily believe the age of miracles has returned," said the Prince ; "this is a grandmother's apple-pie and no mistake."

"Undoubtedly it is," said the Princess.

"And who made it ?" asked the Prince.

"I made it," said the Princess.

There are feelings as we all know, and have been taught, which cannot be expressed in words. The Prince's mouth was full; his heart was full; it was only necessary to complete his happiness that his plate should be full. He said nothing, but helped himself to the rest, residue, and remainder of the pie.

" You seem to be playing the 'grab game' on my pie," said the Little Lady, gaily.

"Yes," said the Prince, "I have an 'attachment' for it."

And he laughed, heartily, at this little joke, and so did they all. Not because there was the least merit in the joke, but because, when people are in high good humor, they will laugh at almost anything.

The Little Lady had her own quiet source of

amusement, in the belief, in the very depths of **her** honest **heart**, that the Prince's grandmother had **never**, in the whole course of her long and exemplary life, made a pie half as good as her own, but **she** was satisfied with things **as** they were, and perfectly willing to be placed, by the Prince, in a niche on the same level with his grandmother, in his Walhalla, or special shrine, of famous pie-makers.

# CHAPTER XIII.

AMONG the votaries and high priestesses of that all-powerful divinity, Societas, none were more conspicuous in the Imperial City than the Princess Gloriosa. Older by only a couple of years than Prima, she was a millenium in advance of her in all the ways of the world. Brought up together as playmates and schoolmates, Gloriosa had married, at an early age, and was soon established as a recognized social power, by virtue of her beauty, her wit, her vivacity, her force of will, and the supposed wealth of her husband, Novus, a daring and adventurous youth, believed to be one of the special favorites of Fortune, and endowed with a faculty kindred to the fabled gift by which Midas could turn everything he touched into gold.

Gloriosa, before her marriage, had known very little about gold, or any other circulating medium, except by description, and that, for the most part, in works of the imagination and fancy. Her widowed mother, whose better days in the past, furnished supplies only for memory and melancholy retrospect, found her sole solace in the possibilities of a splendid future for Gloriosa; and she made every

124

sacrifice to gain for her a firm footing on the slippery pathway into the sanctuary of **the** gilded goddess. **Once** initiated, she needed no support **from other** votaries, or fellow-worshipers. She **was a** ready adept in all the arts and graces which were **needed** for the service in which she had engaged, and when Novus, with all his rapidly made wealth, was wedded to Gloriosa, with all her speedily acquired prominence, there was a general feeling **in** the charmed circle that the race had indeed been to the swift, **and that a** rightful **leadership had** been established.

The Little Lady had permitted, if not encouraged, **a** continuance **of** the **early intimacy between the** two friends, partly, because **it offered to Prima some** opportunities **of** enjoyment, **of which she** might otherwise have been deprived, and partly, **because her** nature was so retiring and contemplative that **it** needed something of the stimulus which the ardent world-wisdom of Gloriosa was calculated **to** impart.

Prima, **at this time, coeval** with the outbreak of the strife **for the Sisterhood, was** nearly out **of her** teens; **to** borrow **the charming refrain of a stray song, in a** noble English drama :—

> "She was fresh **and** she was fair,
> Glossy was her golden hair,
> Like a blue spot in the sky,
> Was her clear and loving eye."

**And** yet opinions differed as **to her** claim to beauty. Many critics, of her own sex, denied **it absolutely.**

She lacked height; she lacked pose; she had fault-less teeth, but her mouth was too large; her features were irregular, her nose was not of the true classic type; and what so many people found in her to admire, they could not, for their lives, divine. The claim to rank as a beauty was one which Prima had never dreamed of asserting on her own behalf, nor had she the least suspicion that it was put forward by anyone in her interest, and she would have been greatly surprised had she come to the knowledge that it was, in fact, a vexed question, stirred with many cups of afternoon tea, and often started afresh at the moment of her entrance into some gay scene, where the rites of Societas were in festal progress.

Gloriosa, however, was never tired of declaring that Prima was "simply perfect," and this was the true verdict of the majority of voices apt to echo her own. But, in the same breath, she would admit that Prima would never shine as a satellite in the bright, planetary system of Societas. In spite of her opportunities, she would not dance to all the piping of the priestesses. Cinderella's slipper would have cut no figure on her dainty foot. The cardinal doctrine of Societas, that all youth and beauty are predestinated to the round dance, by inevitable decree, she heretically rejected, and while Gloriosa mourned over her defection, consigning her, more in sorrow than in anger, to the penal sufferance and durance vile of the slow-footed sect of the wall-flowers, she still hovered and buzzed over her, like a magnificent and many-colored butterfly above a wee, modest, field flower.

Gloriosa herself was a full-orbed beauty, of a somewhat aggressive type. She was taller than Prima; she filled more space; her voice was pitched on a higher key; her eyes were more of a Juno gray than of the true cerulean blue; her luxuriant tresses wore a heavier imprint than the golden-tinted locks of Prima, and seemed of a somewhat baser metal. She was, generally, of a larger pattern, and her views were on a correspondingly liberal scale. She was indefatigable in the discharge of her duties, in the service of Societas. Her responsibilities were simply enormous. Her visiting list was like a Bank Ledger. Her engagements were scheduled and tabulated with the precision of a Bureau of Statistics. Her entertainments were organized with the detail of a military campaign. She had a vast army of subordinates, from the humblest camp-follower, who was glad to get an occasional card for a fifth-rate reception, to her staff officers, who led the Grecian in every gay saloon, and whose gilded chariots waited before her palace gates.

To tell the plain truth, if ever there was a false goddess and sham divinity, it was this same Societas. Time was, when her shrine and her service meant something of value to the community, as well as to her immediate votaries. In those earlier days, her precincts were guarded closely and with jealous care. Moat and drawbridge had to be passed, portcullis raised, and watchword duly given, before access could be gained to her citadel, or her sanctuary, nor could any one be admitted to her higher mysteries and privileges without due scrutiny, and test, and full performance of all required lustrations. But now, the ancient landmarks had been rudely broken down, and the great sacred circle of Societas came to resemble the modern circus tent, where every one is welcome who can pay the entrance money, and a penniless straggler, now and then, contrives to crawl in under the flap. The decay dated from the time when, by an edict issued in her name, the test of admission to her inner courts was changed from weight of character to weight of purse, and soon thereafter a wild horde of new-made plutocrats, covered with the slime of Pactolus, came trampling into the sacred enclosure.

The great aim of the worship of Societas, as organized by her votaries, was to destroy whatever was natural, and replace it by whatever was artificial. They registered vows to substitute the conventional for the true, and their whole lives were devoted to this end with the all-consuming energy of zealots. They had no written code, but their prescripts, like the Common Law of England, were a vast body of rules, understood by those who enforced them, applied according to their own interpretation, and, very largely, embedded in customs as inviolate as law. Thus the declaration at the door of a patrician dame to an inquiring visitor— " Not at home "—was a conventionalism, which, being interpreted, meant that she **was at** home, but **did not** choose to admit visitors. This serviceable **con-trivance** we may easily suppose to have been origin-**ated by** Domesticus, who drew **his sustenance** largely **from** Societas, because it gave **him such a** safe precedent for carrying a convenient amount of conventionalism **into** butlers' pantries, and other places, **and** laying his deflections from truth **at the** front door **of his mistress.**

Having thus caused Truth to fall in the street, **or** on the front steps leading thereto, she was easily defeated everywhere else. In current interchanges of civility; in the acceptance **or regret of proffered** hospitality; **in the exchange of courtesies; in the** bestowal **of** gifts; **in** the endless round **of commu-**nications, the great **law of** conventionality **was supreme.** From this lower grade of purely human affairs, the ascent to open hostility against the established **order** of Nature was easy. Societas, **like** Milton's Satan, hated the sun, and **was as** bent on turning **Night into Day as** ever that **arch enemy** was in **making Evil a substitute for Good. It was one of her prime and absolute requirements that the** best **energies of her followers should be devoted** to this end. **Her high festivities must always begin** about the time that **the** human race, in general, **wants** to go to bed, and terminate a little before **the time** appointed to the sons of men to rise and go forth **to their daily** labor. To this law everything must be **sacrificed; the peace** and order **of** families; **the bloom and beauty** of maidenhood; **the** vigor **and**

9

strength of early manhood. True, the fair votaress
might float away, in her gossamer wraps, in the
small morning hours, to unbroken slumber protracted to midday, and deem this a full equivalent
for the rejected sleep which the night had proffered, a delusion, sure to be dispelled sooner or
later, perhaps too late. True, her attendant cava-
lier might think his stock of strength enabled him
to make the brief rest—caught between the end of
the night's revel and the beginning of the day's
work—suffice to furnish him for the exactions of his
calling, or, if exempt from labor, he might suppose
that in the vacuity, or idleness, or varied sports of
the daytime, he could recruit his energies for the
ever-recurring, nightly treadmill of gayety. But, in
reality, the whole system was a long crusade
against Nature and natural law, kept up with ceaseless vigilance and fanatical zeal by the standing
army of Societas, whose veterans, decorated with
diamonds and lace, tottered in the glare of the midnight lamps, and whose recruits, bright with the
radiance of youth, were willing to risk everything
in her perilous service.

"Why cannot people enjoy themselves at reasonable hours?" said Prima, one day, to Gloriosa,
when she made her an unusually early visit, and
the conversation had begun with a glowing account
of a recent high festival of Societas. "You wonder
that I avoid your grand crushes. It is not because
I do not like being among so many people—on
the contrary—I find a vast deal of amusement and

entertainment, but I am an absentee, simply and solely, because I prefer to be abed and asleep between midnight and morning.

" My dear Prima, you talk like a Spartan grandmother. Would you do your dancing by daylight?"

"No," said Prima, "but the very little dancing I do, I should like the privilege of doing before bedtime. It may be Spartan grandmotherliness, but more than half the ways of Societas seem to me not only absurd, but absolutely wrong."

" Go on, Prima, you look so pretty when you are preaching."

" I can't help it if I do, but if ever I had an authentic call to preach, I should not waste it on you or any of the case-hardened, high-heeled priestesses. I only wish you had sense enough for a new departure. You could do a world of good, and make yourself immortal, if you had the will and the courage to head a revolution against these destructive, unnatural hours, but I know you will never do it."

" Never, indeed! the very thought of such a thing is high treason; the first vow of my novitiate bound me to renounce everything reasonable, natural, and sensible, where it contravened the edicts of Societas, and I mean to live up to my professions. But, my precious Prima, I came this morning on a special errand, from which our discussion must not divert me. Who is this Juventus I am hearing so much about?"

With this question, Gloriosa darted a keen, inquisitive glance at Prima. Her shot, whether at a venture or with deliberate aim, hit the mark, if blushes are a true index, and it was followed by a second, before Prima had rallied from the effect of the first.

" Is it true that he is a machinist and works in a factory ? "

" He works for his living, as most men do, who are of any account."

" But does he work for wages, like ordinary laborers—like Domesticus ? "

" I suppose," said Prima, very quietly, having regained entire self-possession, " he works for pay, just as the ediles, and prætors, and jurisconsults, do. Why not ? "

" Oh, certainly, the laborer is worthy of his hire. It was his social measure I wanted to take, and to ascertain, if I could, how he came to find favor in your blue eyes. Did he come here to mend the water pipes or tune the organ pipes ? "

" He came here to dinner, on papa's invitation, with the other wizards of the Imperial Society for the Maintenance of the Solar System. You know about them, I presume ? "

" Oh, yes, they walk in the clouds and discourse about the sun. They maintain a great deal of eating, and drinking, and discussing, but I don't believe it affects the solar system the least bit."

" Very well, papa had them to dinner, and Juventus, being the youngest wizard, took me out."

" And then, presumably, you had cube roots for

*hors d'œuvres,* and conic sections for a *pièce de résistance.*"

"No, we talked about a great many things, much more interesting, your sweet self for example, and I told him the story of your symposium when the lady guests pocketed the gold salt-cellars, at their plates, on the pretext that, like favors at the Grecian, they were to be reduced to possession, and carried off, at the close of the entertainment."

"An excellent story," said Gloriosa, "to be taken with as many grains of salt as there were in the salt-cellars. Not a word of truth in it. But, certainly, I can afford to have it told if my guests can, and to be talked about is the first step toward fame. To become a dinner table topic is half the battle."

"And you are always my favorite topic. I described to him your Etruscan room, which is so far in advance of everything, but I didn't dare tell him how much the ceiling cost."

"If it ever needs repairing, I will send for him. Tell me, Prima, do you know anything about his antecedents? What are his belongings? Who are his people?"

"His people are ship builders, way off, on the coast of Dirigo."

"Oh, a mechanic and the son of a mechanic!"

"Yes, but he is not an ordinary mechanic. He is very highly educated."

"So is my chef," said Gloriosa, "he speaks three languages, and cooks in seven, and, I dare say, has higher wages than your prodigy, who may be a wonderful workman and a wonderful wizard, but we cannot let down the bars for such as he."

"There is certainly no need," said Prima. "He is inside already."

"It is quite out of the question," persisted Gloriosa, "a working-man may have all the education you please; it will help him in his place and, perhaps, help him to rise from it; but as long as he stays in it, how can he possibly have any social position?"

"Surely," said Prima, "his education entitles him to position, just as much, if not a great deal more, than the money of a rich man who can hardly write or spell his own name. Besides, there is a vast difference in work. His is not menial or servile, in any sense, but of the highest kind, requiring brain and talent, and even genius, like the work of the old-time bridge-builders. What does Pontifex Maximus mean except the greatest of bridge-builders?"

"That is all very fine, if we are to go back a thousand years, or so. I dare say the mound-builders were equally distinguished in their day and generation, but the kind of worth that makes the man, now, is not his being able to work, but his being able to do without work. Societas has settled all that, and she will rule out Juventus. No gentleman works with his hands."

"Then I renounce all my allegiance to Societas," said Prima, with unwonted spirit in her tone and look. "What is there to-day of any real value, except labor, or what labor has created? Did you ever think, Gloriosa, that if the men and women who do the work of the world, outdoors and indoors, were, all at once, to stop working, the whole race would starve, as soon as they had eaten up what was left in the larders? A gold heap or a silver heap would be no better then than a dust heap. You are living every moment by some one's labor and yet you despise the laborer. I will take back what I said about differences in work. All work is good, and true, and noble, if the aim and the end are right."

Gloriosa thought she could divine the possible source of Prima's heretical declarations, but she was in earnest when she said that she liked to hear her preach, and so she chose to fan the flame she had kindled.

"And when this somewhat improbable catastrophe takes place, and everybody stops working all at once (except Juventus, for, if he is what you paint him, I suppose he will keep on all the same), what particular branch of industry do you propose to take up?"

"Oh, I will come and teach you plain sewing and ever so many other useful arts," said Prima, frightened at her little flight into the region of political economy, and making haste to get back to the proper level of parlor platitudes.

"Prima," said Gloriosa, solemnly, "I really and truly believe you are in love with Juventus. You must promise me one thing, on your sacred word and honor. If he asks you to marry him, say 'No.'"

"But I have said 'Yes' already."

"When?" shrieked Gloriosa.

"Yesterday," said Prima.

"Unhappy girl! It was only yesterday I heard he was going to the war."

"So he is."

"And when may that be?"

"To-morrow," said Prima.

There was a pause. Gloriosa was quick of wit, and her thoughts came and went with rapidity. If Juventus were going to the war, he might be killed, or he might come back at the head of a legion. In either case, he would be a hero. It was a chance for an epitaph or a brace of epaulettes. A military record would wipe out the stain of the workshop. At all events, Prima would have her own way, and why not make a virtue of necessity, and take them both under her protecting wing.

Prima, meanwhile, was more stunned by her own announcement than the friend to whom it had been made. She was barely regaining full consciousness, when she felt herself in the tight embrace of Gloriosa, whose stout arms, encased in their many-buttoned gloves, were clasped about her, and their reunited hearts were again beating in unison, as they basked in the glow of that incommunicable rapture with which the secret of a fresh engagement never fails to suffuse the spirit of the gentler sex.

# CHAPTER XIV.

WHAT Prima told Gloriosa was the whole truth. Juventus had found a friendly reception and a continuing welcome under the roof of the Prince, from the time of his first introduction, in the train of the scientists.

He soon became a favored guest.

The Princess had seen him render a casual act of courtesy, in a public place, at some personal inconvenience, to an elderly dame, and this incident, even more than his deferential bearing toward herself, gave him an exceptional standing in her good opinion, in view of the lamentable decline, which she affirmed to exist, in the respect paid by youth to age.

The Prince liked his coming, because, as he said, the young man always told him something he did not know before.

Secundus, the bright princelet of the family, was helped by Juventus out of many of the snares and pitfalls, filled with deceptive signs and delusive figures, into which the pedagogues delighted to lead unwary youthful adventurers in the path of knowledge.

137

He had won the heart of little Tertia by a marvelous restoration of the scattered members of her favorite doll, after a catastrophe which had seemed fatal to its curiously contrived existence.

Even more than to any one else in the household, was he an object of admiration, almost of worship, to Stella, the special ministrant with whom Domesticus had invested Prima. She thought Juventus had saved her life. In fact, he had stepped opportunely, between her and possible, if not probable, death. As he was going his round in one of the workshops, where she tended a machine, a sudden break threw the mechanism out of gear, and she was in danger of being caught and fearfully maimed in the whirl of the disorganized and destructive mass. Juventus, by a sudden and timely act, had snatched her from this dangerous plight, just at the moment of a crash which might have been fatal. This accident so affected her nervous system that she could not safely return to machine work, and when he told the story to the Princess, she made a place for the girl in her household. She waited on Prima, giving a great deal of uninstructed, but willing service, and a great deal of trouble in her unregulated methods of mind and manners, but, in spite of all these shortcomings, finding sympathy in the kind hearts of her mistresses.

To Prima, Juventus seemed unlike most young men, and this, she thought, was all she thought about him.

Meanwhile, Juventus found himself thinking more and more about Prima, until, after the old fashion whereby human hearts are entwined and human destinies interwoven, there was nothing in the wide universe for him, in sentiment, in resolve, in action; in the seeing of the eye, the hearing of the ear, the imagining of the heart, which did not seem to draw its vital breath from this bright ideal. His plans and purposes found a new inspiration and a new motive, and he seemed to himself to have come, all at once, within a single step of the summit of happiness.

Juventus, as he worked and walked, and slept and waked, carried with him this thought of Prima, which he could not dissever from another and earlier thought, whose first access had filled him with an intense ardor, kindred to that which now stirred his soul with the throbbings of a new affection. To the love of country, this added love seemed only a later and more perfect outgrowth from one native stock. The same chord of his nature vibrated to the touch of loyalty and love.

At last, out of a myriad of glimmering, confused, and intermingled certainties and uncertainties, and hopes and fears, vast and vague as the unresolved nebulæ of Andromeda, a clear and bright resolve fashioned itself in his mind, and was wrought into shape as follows:—

" JUVENTUS TO PRIMA, Greeting:

" It has been the desire of my heart, ever since

that first firing on the flag, to volunteer and go to the front.

"When the great Flamen, whose words have always been as oracles to me, declared that the strife would be ended in sixty days, I was willing to wait. Now, that it seems as if the truer prophecy was that other word, for uttering which a brave man was sneered at as a lunatic, that three hundred thousand men would be needed to save the Sisterhood, I must be one of them. The call seems plain to me, and there are some good and true men who will also go, if I go. And I must go at once, if at all. The one thing I want to carry with me is your heart. A man who in facing danger, perhaps death, and who turns his back on a career just entered upon, and a livelihood barely secured, has, I know full well, no right to ask the sacrifice I solicit from you, even could he count on the affection which might make it possible. Yet I must venture all, knowing that you have courage and faith, and believing that I can make you happy, if only you can return my love.

" Do not write ; I will come this evening."

The earlier portion of this missive told no news to Prima. She had known, well enough, that Juventus would go to the war. She had hoped this and feared it, and feared it and hoped it, and then tried, in vain, to persuade herself that she neither feared nor hoped it, nor in fact cared at all—and yet she was certain he would go.

The latter part of the letter was a genuine surprise. She had not brought herself to the point of looking on Juventus as a lover. She only knew that she was happy in his society, that she looked forward, with pleasure, to his coming, that she missed his absence, and that was all, absolutely all.

Nevertheless, there was not an instant of doubt in her heart, as to her response. To have the love of a brave, true soul, such as his, was a treasure in itself, and a warrant for all risks. Prima did not hesitate or delay. She sat, for a few minutes, in the stillness of her happy thoughts, and then went to her mother, placed the letter in her hands and knelt before her. Presently, there was a locked embrace; a beating of hearts close to one another; and a season of silent weeping, which he may attempt to describe who can analyze a mother's tears, or fathom the depths of a daughter's love.

That night Juventus came, and as the slight figure of Prima, in spotless white, moved towards him through the dimly lighted space which she seemed to fill with sudden radiance, almost before he could discern her features he caught sight of the blended colors in the silken girdle which bound her waist, the red, white and blue. He asked nothing more. This mute, inarticulate "yes," breathed in the symbol of the cause he was going forth to serve, gave him the answer for which he had hardly dared to hope, and with the confirming clasp of the tiny, trembling hand he rushed forward to claim as his own, no word was needed, and no word was given.

The Prince was somewhat slow to acquiesce in the arrangements of the young people. He thought the whole thing was premature. In a general way, he believed in the future of Juventus, just as he believed in the eventual success of a great many enterprises which yielded no immediate return. He was opposed to his going to the war, because, in reality, he was opposed to the war; but he knew that he could no more stop him than he could hinder the great rivers, which flowed past the Imperial City, from emptying into the ocean.

He could not help thinking the war needless. It should have been prevented, in some way, he did not know how. He was afraid it would be a failure. He doubted whether it would be worth what it cost. Of course, he was for maintaining the Sisterhood. There was no other alternative, but like so many of his class in private stations and so many in public positions, he was in opposition to every measure to maintain it. He could see nothing certain about the war in its continuance, except its expense, and nothing definite in its results, except disaster. He was not in a frame of mind to take very kindly to what seemed to him to be giving an inopportune preference to sentiment over sound judgment. Still, the time was very short, owing to the necessity of immediate acceptance by Juventus of an offered position which assured him speedy active service. The household party of sentiment seemed to be fully organized and in the ascendant; and he was not the man to stand in the way of plans as to which the Princess and Prima were fully in accord. But, for reasons of his own, he was sorry there was need of haste, and specially sorry for the baleful cause of the haste, the strife of the Sister-hood.

The eve of the departure of Juventus was filled up with many momentous affairs. Going to the front had ceased to be a holiday excursion. It was as serious a business as a man could enter upon, and in spite of the new-found happiness which Juventus and Prima shared, the cloud of the im-pending separation, with its unknown risks and dangers, hung over them.

The children were sorely perplexed. Their satis-faction at having Juventus, with all his wonderful arts, an actual member of the family, was intense. It was like catching a live conjurer and keeping him in a cage. But they were disconsolate at the thought of his leaving them, even though carried off, to their fancy, in a blaze of military glory.

Stella, who had been violent in her rejoicing at a union which she attributed mainly to her own in-cessant prayers for such a result, was ready with certain consecrated amulets and charms which were to render Juventus bullet-proof, sabre-proof, and bomb-proof.

The Prince and Princess were busied with many and various thoughts of their own, and Juventus and Prima found the evening hours too short for what it was in their hearts to say. They made as many prom-ises, and protestations, and plans, as could be crowded into the fast flying moments, and wasted some precious time, rather foolishly, but prettily, in selecting, out of all the twinkling stars with which the sky was sprinkled, one bright particular orb, in respect whereof they would bind themselves, by solemn league and covenant, that toward it, on every night whereon it should be visible and within their range of vision, their gaze should be directed, and a last goodnight exhaled. Many stars were successively put in nomination for this high choice, and after an active canvass, the unanimous suffrages of the lovers fell, at last, on the North Star, as best symbolizing the constancy, devotion, and singleness of aim, which entered into the sentiments to be breathed from these two devoted spirits, from their separate places on this little planet, toward its distant polar sphere.

The leave-taking of Juventus finished, and his last adieu given, the Prince walked with him, a short distance, along the broad avenue, and on parting, said, with an unwonted tremor in his voice—

"My dear boy, we shall hope to hear only good news from you. You must be prepared to hear some news from me which may not be good."

"I trust," said Juventus, recalling a chance word of Prima as to the depressed spirits of her father, "there is no illness, of which I have not been told."

"No, I am well enough," said the Prince, "but there are business troubles I may not be able to surmount. I cannot tell yet. It is this which has made me seem less ready to accede to your plans than might otherwise have been the case. Prima's future may be seriously affected."

"If I can deserve your good esteem," said Juventus eagerly, "and if you are willing to trust her future with me, this is all I ask."

The Prince pressed his hand and turned back. He went into the deserted and darkened parlor, and sat alone for several hours, not going up stairs to his bed room, until near the dawn of morning. The Princess did not know of this, or miss his coming. She was with Prima, who had not known, until the final farewell, what parting meant, when, with the sorrow of separation, it mingled the dark forebodings born of the terrors of a cruel and bloody war.

10

# CHAPTER XV.

## A BAD NAME.

THE dire threat and malediction which Decima had hurled, as a Parthian and parting shaft, over the obnoxious apple-pie, at its lovely author, did not spend its force in the air. The bad name she had vindictively promised to give was duly bestowed. The Princess, in her conscious rectitude, and in the quiet pursuit of her daily round of duty, had paid no more attention to the outgivings, than she had to the outgoing, of Decima, having, long ago, learned that nine-tenths of the loud talk of Domesticus was sound and fury, signifying nothing. She did not realize that the giving of a bad name was a kind of final and irreversible anathema and interdict which Domesticus held in reserve for extreme cases, as the old Popes fulminated their bulls of excommunication, by way of firing the last and hottest shot in the well-filled locker out of which they peppered recusant kings, emperors, and non-defenders of the faith.

So, when the Little Lady sallied forth, in her innocence, to consult the sorcerers, and to secure the successor of Decima, in the sphere of the saucepan, she was greatly taken aback by what she encountered. The first shape summoned for her scrutiny no sooner caught sight of her, and surveyed her, than she fled, with a shriek of terror, as if from contact with a leper; while from the murky lurking-place of the ministering spirits, to which she retired, was heard, as through a concerted diapason, a confused murmur of objurgation which fell on the Little Lady's astonished ear like the hissing of the serpents which encircled the head of Medusa.

All the spells of the sorcerer were unavailing. The Little Lady had a bad name. She was under the ban of Domesticus. If he could have his cruel way, no one should ever again give her aid and comfort or service. She might die of hunger; she might perish of thirst; she might be houseless and homeless; but not a morsel of bread, not a drop of water, not a helping hand, should be afforded her by him or his.

What she was reported, in these imprecating depths, and by these wickedly wagging tongues, to have done, to mark her out for this brand of Domesticus, was something of which even Decima, when she set on foot her revengeful outcry, had not dreamed. The utmost that she charged against the Little Lady was that she had, by a single wrongful and malicious act, robbed an apple-pie of its bottom crust, and a poor girl of a month's wages, and that, with one blow of her high hand, she had evicted the lemon from its lawful homestead in the heart of the pie, and turned an honest woman out of doors.

This was bad enough, but as the accusation was

caught up and tossed from willing tongues to greedy ears, along the endless whispering gallery which Domesticus had constructed, and in which his followers waited, it grew apace, and to frightful proportions. The Little Lady had invented and practiced unheard-of cruelties. She was the woman who had driven away the lady who did her cooking. She was subject to spasms of insane hatred against Domesticus. It was unsafe to come under her roof. She kept her household at the starving point. She allowed no rest or respite, not a day, or an hour off, or an evening out. She had ordered a good-looking and inoffensive young parcel clerk of a respectable grocer, out of the house, with fierce denunciation, simply because he wanted to spend the entire morning with the housemaids. She had forbidden card-parties, below stairs. She had emptied a flagon into the sink, with her own hands, because she declared that it was falsely labeled cough mixture, which it was, but for all that no lady would have done it. She had brained several unoffending persons with the rolling pin, and if her premises should be searched there was no telling what might be found; and even if old Tremens should tell all he knew about the ghosts that went up and down the cellar stairs, in the dead of night, when he kept the house one summer, the mansion would soon be marked by the avengers "and made a howling heap, it would."

This time, however, Domesticus had overshot the mark. True, he had a momentary triumph. The

Little Lady was obliged to retire, ignominiously, and with a sense of leaving pointed fingers, and cruel calumnies, and derisive epithets, behind her, and she felt as though she were doing penance, in public, for some heinous crime. The humiliation was only for a very short time, and it was followed, on her part, by a healthful reaction of good humor. If Domesticus had only found food for derision in her honest, though futile efforts at economic rule, during the brief episode of her weights and measures, she now, in her turn, found only amusement and a sense of whimsical pity at this ebullition of his wrath, which, in reality, did her no more harm than the fierce looks of the stiff-jointed old giant who sat in his cave and grinned at Christian, on his way to the Celestial City, did to that valiant pilgrim.

She came home, as from a matinée at the Amphitheatre, and recounted her experience to Prima, who was, at first, a little frightened.

"I declare," she said, "this is outrageous. It is all Decima's doings. Cannot papa have that dreadful woman arrested? To set on foot such slanders must surely be a crime to be punished by the judges."

"If all the people, high and low, who slander other people were to be arrested," replied the Princess, with a wonderful access of wisdom, " the judges would have their hands so full with them that all other criminals would go scot free. Once upon a time, such a thing as this would have made me feel dreadfully, and I should have had several crying spells over it, but the tender grace of a day that is dead, if it was a grace, belongs to that remote period, and I have grown as tough as a knot of gnarled oak."

"But if they won't live with you, mamma, what are we going to do?"

"This gust will blow itself out," said the Princess. "So many other mistresses will be given bad names that, by and by, they won't be able to remember who are on the black list and who are off it."

"Why not do as the Princess Prompta told us, the other day, she does?" said Prima. "She captures new arrivals at the shore end of the ship's gang-planks, who cannot speak or understand, a word of our mother tongue, and gets them into her service, before Domesticus has a chance to put his clutches on them, and then she teaches them everything herself."

"Yes, but didn't you hear the story she told of the foreign virago, over six feet tall, who, when, at the end of the first month, her ten sestertia were paid her, held up ten bony fingers, three times, in succession, and poured forth such a volley of Norse or Runic, or some other unknown tongue, that she had to give her all the money she had in the house, and a silk dress, and ever so much imitation lace besides."

"I suppose we must send for old Patella," said Prima.

"I sent for her, before I came up stairs," said the Princess.

"Old Patella" was a stand-by of the family, of the rank and file of Domesticus, who having been generously helped, in the poverty of her early days, by the Princess, as well as kept in her service, had graduated to the degree and dignity of day-work and lived in a secluded altitude of her own, whence she descended to assist her patrons, as occasion required. She had been a hard-working, indefatigable woman, skillful with her scrubbing-brush, and able to turn her hand to almost any department of service. Besides which she was reputed to have saved all she had earned, beyond her very frugal needs and the due stipend paid at the shrine of her devotions.

"What should we do," the Prince had often said, "if we were not sure that old Patella is praying for us, night and day?"

"A brilliant idea strikes me," said Prima; "if you are under the ban of Domesticus, why not teach Stella to cook? She is wonderfully bright, only her intelligence always seems to be about the wrong thing. It would be a good plan to concentrate it on the culinary art."

"I must leave Stella to you," said the Princess. "I have got beyond trying to teach the rudiments."

"But, mamma, how many, and how much, you have taught."

"I know I have, and perhaps that is really the way in which I have learned to do for myself. The teacher's best pay is very often what he gains from the instruction he gives to others. I might, even now, be willing to teach what I know, to any one wanting to learn, but unteachableness is the badge of the whole race to which Stella belongs."

"Still, we can't send her away, and why may not I try the experiment? I will get all the new receipt books and cooking books, and she is a good reader and has real taste; perhaps I can really and truly help you, more than you think, and then, you know, according to what you have just said, even if the pupil learns nothing, the teacher may learn something."

"It will be the blind leading the blind, I fear," said the Princess, "but you may make any venture you please with Stella."

Prima was an adept at higher instruction, as she was with her needle, and in various arts requiring skill and dexterity of hand. This was her first excursion into the perilous region she proposed to explore, in her new capacity of guide and pioneer, with Stella as her sole follower, but she was determined to try her fortune in the fresh field.

The science of dietetics was now approached on the side of the intellect and the imagination. Prima invested some irrecoverable sums in ponderous volumes, which were to the new subject of her study what the Pandects and Digests were to the body of the law. They codified the whole vast science and reduced it to a perfect system. Here were diagrams of prize bullocks, and fatted calves, and trussed fowls, all exhibited with lines, and letters, and figures, in an attractive simplicity, such as on the pages of Euclid charm the eye of the beginner in geometry.

Prima, as she pursued her studies, and took in not only these guide books and digests of the art, but explored its wider range, was amazed at the learning which had been lavished on the culinary art; at the great names which were identified with its triumphs; the memories it enshrined, and the history it had created. It was the earliest handmaid of hospitality, when men entertained angels unawares. It was coeval with the sacred ties of friendship, and the first altar-fires of devotion. It was interwoven with the threads of classic song and story; with the rude legends of barbaric races; with the whole stately growth of Civilization. It was the ceaseless strengthener of brain and muscle; the great stay of human labor; the promoter of genial intercourse; the source of inexhaustible wit, and humor, and high discourse; the foster-mother of all the fair humanities. And yet, was it not in many aspects, a lost art; and where, oh where, was the plastic touch at which it would re-assert its rightful place, and be once more a benefaction in the homes of men!

Prima, arrayed in her panoply of literature, and Stella, in her illiterate nakedness, plunged into the breakers, and were, of course, taken very far out to sea by the undertow of their absolute ignorance. They began by attempting the most difficult dishes, and ended by a waste of raw material unparalleled in the domestic economy of the Princess. It was

as if a tyro in the rudiments of drawing had undertaken to make a prize copy of the Laocoon.　At
the nearest point of success, in one of their simplest endeavors, Prima left Stella to watch the seemingly favorable conditions to which they had brought
the compounded elements of a projected pudding,
in order that she might finish a letter to Juventus.
During her absence, the strains of martial music,
indicating the passing of a legion on its way to the
distant front of the war, drew Stella to the nearer
front of the palace, to shed a few tears and wave a
greeting and farewell; on her return, the utter collapse and irretrievable ruin of the pudding were as
obvious as the traditional fate of the slapjacks
which Alfred the Great forgot to turn, at the critical point of his country's fate.　Stella, in her efforts
to remedy the disaster, contrived to upset a kettle
of hot water upon her blundering self, and was
conveyed, in a scalded condition, to the upper
regions, where Prima had no consolation in tend-
ing her except the thought that she might be learning something which would fit her for hospital service, in case Juventus should have the ill-luck to
come home with a wound.

Practical cooking, from a literary point of view,
having been demonstrated to be a failure, Prima
willingly confessed that she had begun at the wrong
end, and that this department of human effort and
skill, like every other—higher it might be, but not
a whit more needful for human progress—must have
its regular and gradual processes of training and

instruction. First the blade, then the ear, and then the full corn in the ear, is a law of development which common sense will apply as well to the acquisition of the art of cooking the corn as to the art of cultivating it. Minerva might spring, full armed, from the brain of Jove, in the golden age of mythology, but it is unreasonable to expect a white-frocked and white-capped *Chef*, with his array of countless saucepans, to bustle into being out of nothingness, at the whimpering cry of a distressed housewife. Everybody else is trained for their work, everybody else is taught, apprenticed, bound out, articled, or matriculated, but Domesticus has, somehow, set his foot on the rule of growth and tutelage, and established ignorance as the primal and permanent law of his disordered realm.

" Why should not these things which are all so very needful for comfort and happiness, in all homes, high and low, be taught, like other branches?" said Prima to the Princess.

" They ought to be," said the Princess, " and on the same principle, that since you dismounted, so gracefully, or ungracefully, from your very high horse, after Stella had been thrown, you are now, as I notice, taking lessons of old Patella in the simplest mixtures, there should be regularly established schools to teach these useful arts."

" I have been thinking about it," said Prima, " and my high horse, as you call him, will not, I hope, prove a wholly useless animal. I have ridden him fast enough, and far enough, to arrive at some conclusions which I want to compare with your own, and have you tell me whether they are all wrong."

"I dare say they are all quite right, Prima," said the Princess; "I am only glad if you can express them, for the subject is a wonderfully muddling one; and while my convictions are clear to my own mind, I fear I cannot make them plain to any one else."

"What I have thought," said Prima, "is that all these things which relate to household service, up stairs, down stairs, and in my lady's chamber, fall directly into the line of object teaching, and ought to be taught, in that way, and first of all, to children, so as to give the benefit of the teaching in their homes, or half-homes, and to get their hands in. Then, if they go out to service, they can pursue the study, regularly, to fit them for their work, and if they do not, they will know something of house management, and be able to have a certain sense of order and arrangement, which, as you have always said, comes by training and not by nature. Now, of course, we cannot expect to see schools started and equipped, all at once, for these studies, but is it not a good end to aim at, and a field of instruction sooner or later, to be occupied? And why is it not a philanthropic thing, because it would not only help employers, but help working people, if their wives and daughters had the skill to make their dwellings, or their rooms, less dreary and more attractive, by appetizing meals, however humble, and by cleanly, orderly service, however rude?

"I think that is all right and sound, Prima," said the Princess, "I would encourage everything in the way of teaching, and, as you say, it is essentially object teaching, like the instruction in a laboratory. I think every one who attempts this kind of experimental teaching is a benefactor—or a benefactress, —for the teacher, I believe, is almost always a woman; but the difficulty with such instruction, however valuable, so far as Domesticus is concerned, is that his followers have never learned the art of learning, and that is the first and great need. They cannot grasp the thing they are taught, and keep it, or make it their own. And, in general, they do not want to, and won't, and there is the end. My dear Prima, you must catch Domesticus young, very young, to teach him anything. But your plan, of beginning with the children, I like, and there is good in it, to be attempted, if not to be actually accomplished."

"I am happy," said Prima, "that you agree with me. I do not claim any originality in my ideas; they have come from what I have read and heard of other people's doings and efforts, as much as from my own reflections, though, to be fair to myself, the thought was my own, before I found that it was, quite largely, the thought of others. This, I believe is, often, the vindication of the usefulness of an idea, that it enters more minds than one at once. What I want most to know is whether I can do anything myself, in my small way, to help forward the good cause. I can do nothing without you."

"I am with you, heart and soul," said the Princess. "Only let us get through this dreadful strife of the Sisterhood, and have peace, if it is ever to come; and then we will work together in this wide field, even if we can cultivate only a little corner of it. I promise you I will help, in every way I can, in laying the foundation for teaching the untaught art of household service."

The Little Lady never in all her life made a promise which she did not fully keep.

# CHAPTER XVI.

## A CATASTROPHE.

THUNDERBOLTS in clear skies were not infrequent in the Imperial City. There were spirits in the air which kept it full of explosive elements, and which, like the great Destroyer, loved to launch their bolts at shining marks. And yet, the sudden crash which so often startled the community was very apt to be merely the deferred result of causes which had been working, slowly and surely, to the inevitable catastrophe. The unexpected happens only to the unexpectant. The wise men, who had grown gray in casting financial horoscopes, the soothsayers of the money circles, who could discern, on the dilated edge of overtrading, or in the distended bubble of speculation, the signs of impending collapse, could often foresee and foretell the calamities which took the unwary by surprise.

The wise men and the soothsayers had, from the beginning of the war, predicted the downfall of the Prince and his princely house. Their vastly extended dealings on the nether side of the invisible line seemed to make this a foregone conclusion. Their debtors in that wide region were turned, all

at once, into foreign belligerents, without means to
meet their obligations, if they had any longer the
desire to do so, and with their debts all cancelled by
the first cannonade.

The Prince ought to have succumbed at once. He
should have done, as others did who were in similar
plight, and who made no effort to fight against fate,
or to stand up under the crushing weight of a
fratricidal strife. But the Prince thought he was
solvent, whatever might be the outcome of the war.
He had large resources, not involved in his business.
He had bought and paid for a tract of land, within the
limits of the Imperial City, which he owned in his
own right, burdened with no debt, and which, of itself,
he thought, was a guaranty of fortune, although,
being almost wholly unimproved, it yielded no
return. He owned the palace which was his home,
and the great gains of his principality had always
seemed sufficient to make adversity impossible.

Besides, he hugged and cherished the delusion that
the war cloud would soon blow over. He could not
bring himself to believe that when the Sisterhood
found itself really arrayed in arms, and divided
against itself, in hostile camps and with opposing
hosts, the deadly feud would be forced to the issue
of mortal combat. Surely, there would be some
other way than war, and if war came, it might be
only a brush, a drawing of fire, enough fighting to
show that there were brave men on both sides,
and no cowards on either; then the fraternal embrace, and the pipe of peace, and a new welding

of the bonds of union, or an amicable separation and a treaty between two separate sovereignties.

Clinging to these false hopes, he strained every nerve to maintain his credit and to meet all his obligations, and having powerful friends and allies beyond the sea, who had great faith in the Prince's ability, and were in full sympathy with his mistaken ideas, he was able, without selling his lands, or even raising money upon them—which might have injured his standing at home—to carry a brave exterior, to maintain himself as aforetime, and to seem to be outriding the storm.

All at once, and with little premonition, his foreign props failed him. New complications had arisen. The death of the chief of a great house, his principal ally, made necessary the liquidation of its affairs, and the supports he had leaned upon and trusted gave way of a sudden. He was forced to meet, immediately, an overwhelming amount of debt, which all his means were insufficient to discharge. Failure was now inevitable. Rumors flew thick and fast, and were soon followed by the truthful statement, heralded throughout the Imperial City, that the Prince had suspended payment, the mildest form of expression, known to the vernacular of the commercial world, to indicate financial ruin.

The Prince met the blow with such fortitude as he could summon. One thing he determined at the outset of his new and hard experience as an insolvent. All the men whom he owed should fare alike. He would not prefer one to another. All he had

11

should go, equally, to all to whom he was indebted. This, he was sure, was right. Then he winced at the thought that he had wholly failed to make any provision, when he might have made it, for such an emergency as this. Years ago, when he was in the fullest tide of prosperity, when he gave in charity or spent in luxury, in a single twelvemonth, what would now, in his altered state, be almost a competency, why had he not given the palace to the Princess, or made some liberal provision for her, as he might properly have done ? He had never dreamed of this hideous extremity, and now it was too late.

Even the furniture in his house, while it was all bought and added to, with lavish generosity, for her use and enjoyment, he had never formally made over to her, and, aside from the jewels, and trinkets, and wardrobe, which she had in her personal control, and a few scattered articles in the palace, he knew not if there was anything she could call her own. She had no patrimony, her father having, like so many of the citizens of the Imperial City, lived in luxury while his business prospered, but on such a scale that, when he died, its liquidation left only a scant residuum. The Prince had been equally foolish. All that had been his was now only a fund for the payment of his debts. His whole estate must go, at once, into some safe hand, for equal distribution among all the creditors. Already, and before the ink was dry on the parchment which provided for this transfer, one sharpest money dealer had sued out a summary writ, to enforce payment of a dishonored draft, and he was made to feel that, in every way; he was tied, hand and foot, with all the disabilities and disadvantages of a debtor.

He dreaded to go to his own home. The Princess knew that there was difficulty and danger, but he had never been willing to admit to himself, much less to her, the possibility of such an ending as this. Not until the morning of the fatal day, when, like the swift-footed messengers who heaped their successive burdens of evil tidings upon the patriarch of Uz, the post and the electric current brought him the final and fatal missives which wrought his ruin, had he permitted the thought of failure. When he saw it could not be averted, he had sent for the jurisconsults, and in an hour's time, their ready arts had stripped him, with his own free will, of all he possessed, and converted him from a Merchant Prince into a pauper. So, at least, he said bitterly to himself, for, at this moment of his downfall, he felt as if he had nothing left from the past and nothing to look forward to in the future.

He waited until all the formalities were concluded which perfected the transfer of his many properties from himself to one Assignatus, the chosen custodian for the benefit of all his creditors, and then, with a heavy heart, made his way homeward.

He crossed the threshold of his palace—his no longer—and went straight, as his custom was, to the apartment of the Princess, where he had always been sure of a smile and a welcome, whatever storms might be raging without.

He had prepared no phrases in which to set before her the calamity that had befallen him. He could hardly, in his own thoughts, grasp its fearful meaning, much less clothe it in words. What filled him with alarm and terror was the apprehension of the effect the evil tidings might have on her. He thought she would be crushed to the earth; she might be struck senseless and speechless; she might die, and then what should he do? But he could not keep away from her, and when he came into her sight, with a tottering step—for he was almost prostrated by the strain to which he had been subjected during those long morning hours—and with a haggard face, which told the whole sad story, before he had uttered the broken words of which—"ruined"—was all she caught, he was in her embrace, and she was ready with all the aid and comfort a loving heart could give.

"I feared it would come to this," she said, softly, as she made him sit beside her, with his hand in hers, "and now, dearest, I hope it may not be as bad as you have dreaded."

The Princess had not been crushed to the earth, nor struck speechless, nor was she going to die. The Prince's fears for her relieved, turned upon himself again.

"It is as bad as can be. I have lost everything."

" Not your good name, I am sure; not your wife,

for she is beside you ; not your children, for they are all safe at home."

" They will be beggars," said the Prince.

" Not while we have strength to do a day's work for them, or they for us."

" You must give up your chariots and horses," said the Prince.

" It will do us all good to walk."

" We must quit the palace."

"We can be just as happy in a smaller house, and with far less care."

" You will have to do your own housework."

" It will be a real pleasure. We shall have a final riddance of Domesticus."

" You will have a broken-down husband on your hands."

" It will be the sweetest duty of my life to care for him."

" You will be expelled from the circle of Societas."

" We shall have the inner and more sacred circle of home."

" I shall no longer be a Prince."

" Then you will be an ex-Prince," and the Little Lady burst into laughter, for it had always seemed to her, when the Prince introduced her to ex-Consuls, ex-Prætors and ex-Ediles, a most ridiculous thing that the more a man was out of office, the more he held on to any title that had ever belonged to it, as to a kind of perpetual perquisite.

Her laughter was always contagious, and the

Prince could hardly help responding with a smile, but he clung to the dismal shadow which he brought with him into the palace, and he was beginning to feel a little disappointed that the Princess was not enveloped in its black folds as completely as he was himself.

" You really do not seem to care very much for my misfortunes," he said.

" It is because I care for you, so very much more than for all else, good fortune, bad fortune, or anything in the whole world," she said, drawing him still nearer to her, " that I will not be made sad while you and the children are left to me. Wherever we are all together, there will be home, and happiness, whether we have much or little."

Then they sat in silence, for some time.

" You are braver than I," said the Prince, at last, "and I am only too thankful you are not made wretched by this miserable business. Up to last night, I hoped to get through; even this morning, I had offers of help which might possibly have tided us along, perhaps saved us, but the prospect was too gloomy. I have done all I could. Only I reproach myself for not having made provision for you, as I ought to have done. I should have put the palace in your name, years ago. I never anticipated such a time as this. Even the furniture I never made over to you. I suppose, now, everything will have to go to the creditors."

And the Prince looked gloomily around, as if apprehensive that some of them were waiting, in

the second-story hall, to carry off the sofa on which
he and the Princess were sitting, in their sorrow.

"No matter for that," said she in a cheery tone.
"We shall not want much, and you will be surprised to see how I can make a very little go a great
ways. At all events, I am not going to be miserable and disconsolate, until there is positively nothing else to be done."

"You are sure you are not putting all this on,
just to keep me up," said the poor Prince, still
clinging to the shadow.

"Perfectly sure," said the Princess, rising and
standing before him, her whole presence taking on
an air of dignity he had never seen so marked before,
"I am as honest in this as I have always been, in
everything. Did I not take you for richer or
poorer, and of what use am I, if, when poverty
comes, I cannot help you bear it? I do not care
how bad things may be. Your home shall always
be happy, if my heart and hands can make it so.
All I ask is your love, to make my labor light."

"That shall never fail you," said the Prince,
rising in his turn, and clasping her in his arms,
"only I can not forgive myself for my own folly and
want of foresight. And what a sad change for
Prima and Juventus."

"It may be the best thing in the world for both
of them," said the Princess, and the Prince—finding
it was quite impossible to break down her good
spirits—yielded himself to her gentle ministrations,
and to her efforts to change the current of his

thoughts into the quiet channel of customary things. Prima and the children were soon about him, with their bright faces, and before bed time he was disposed to take such comfort as he could in their cheerful companionship, and as a last resource would fain console himself with the traditional saying of one of the wisest, and the wealthiest, of the old-time millionaires of the Imperial City, that all he could ever get for himself out of his fortune was three meals a day, and a night's lodging.

In fact, the tragical disclosure of the Prince had not come upon the Little Lady entirely without foreboding on her part. She had noted his anxieties, and he had plainly enough expressed his apprehensions of trouble, although in so vague a way as not to excite immediate alarm. She had, however, nerved herself for disaster, should it come, and now that the storm had burst, she felt strong enough to brave its fury. In the depth of her heart was a sense of conscious courage to grapple with adverse fortune, as bravely as when she fought her battle with Domesticus, and there was a source of satisfaction in feeling that she could be, more than ever, sovereign in her own sphere when circumscribed and contracted by necessity; for she well knew that the comforts and luxuries of life are rarely relinquished from choice.

The revelation of the Prince also explained a mysterious occurrence of the morning, which she had awaited his coming to elucidate, but now she was satisfied, without clearly understanding it any

better, that it had reference to the catastrophe he
announced, and she did not trouble him with any
questions. She had been away from home most of
the day, on a visit to a friend, who was ill, and at
whose bedside she was kept for several hours. On
her return, Patella had come, in considerable excitement, to tell her that two men who called themselves
deputy-somethings, she could not remember what,
had come to the palace, insisted on entering, made
themselves very free indeed, and said they had put a
levy on the furniture, and it covered the whole of it;
but after they had gone away she looked all over
the furniture, and could not find a scrap of new
covering, or anything else on it. She was sure they
said "levy," because they said it over and over a
great many times.

The Princess had heard of levying war, and levying taxes, but she had never heard of a levy on furniture, and thought Patella must have made a mistake.

"What kind of men were they?"

Patella said they were very polite and gentle-
manly, but looked· as if they were a kind it would
be safer to keep out of a house, before they got into
it, than to try to put out, after they were once in.

This was rather vague, in the way of description,
but it had to suffice, and the Princess could only
wait until evening and then she kept silence, lest
the Prince's trouble should be made greater. He
had said the furniture must all go to the creditors,
and she could not see that it mattered whether it
went with a levy on it, or just as it was.

# CHAPTER XVII.

## RIGHT AND WRONG OF DOWER.

IT seemed a strange thing to the Prince that, for the first time in many weeks, he should enjoy a long and unbroken rest during the night which followed the day of his failure. He had retired early, and did not wake until long after his accustomed hour for rising. The sleep which care had driven from his pillow, while he thought and planned to keep his property, came back, with healing in its wings, as soon as he had lost it. He woke with that vague sense of unreality which will often possess the brain after a long, sound slumber, and it was some time before he could recall the consciousness of his impoverished condition, which was now to abide with him in all his waking hours.

He found the Princess and Prima at the breakfast table, the younger children having gone already to their daily tasks at school. He was greeted with unusual warmth and cheerfulness.

"Here are many kind words from old friends," said the Princess, handing him some missives she had received, expressing regrets and sympathies for the sudden misfortunes of the Prince, "and Gloriosa has written to Prima that the gates of Societas are not to be closed upon her, without due notice, and proposing to take her to the seashore, or some-where, for the Summer, so that she may have plenty of gayety to distract her mind, and keep it from dwelling too much on Juventus, in his perils, or on you, in your anxieties."

"She is a frivolous woman," said the Prince, sen-tentiously.

"But she has a good heart under all her frivolity," said the Princess, "and she really loves Prima."

"There is no question about that," said Prima, "and her invitation is just as kindly intended as it is absolutely out of place, and beyond acceptance. I will write and decline it."

"And give her my love," said the Princess.

"And mine, I suppose," said the Prince, who was becoming more amiable, as he sipped his coffee and began on a second chop, somewhat surprised to find that everything had not lost its flavor, and become absolutely noxious to sight and sense.

"Father Vindex is waiting to see you," said the Princess, "he has stopped, on his way to his busi-ness, and was very glad to hear you were resting. He said he had plenty of time, and you were to finish your breakfast."

Vindex, to whom the Princess gave the title of Father, on account of his age and the respect in which he was held, was a gray-headed and long-headed jurisconsult, versed in all the learning of the law and its intricate methods. The Prince had long been on terms of friendly intimacy with him, and often counseled with him in various matters of importance; in the present emergency he had been called in only at the moment when the crisis had arrived, and when immediate action was required. He had then but little opportunity of talking with the Prince about his affairs, and hence his early visit at the palace.

He went at once to the topic of which their thoughts were full.

"My good friend," he said, taking the Prince by the hand, "you had a hard day, yesterday, but things will come out all right in the end."

The Prince shook his head mournfully, and absolutely refused to be comforted by any such smooth prophecy.

"We shall see," said Vindex, "in the meantime, it is very fortunate that there is a ready way of making good provision for your wife and children."

"How is that?" asked the Prince, "this is my greatest regret, that I neglected to make provision myself, when I had it in my power."

"You stand all the better with the creditors for not having done so. They are all friendly, except that pestilent fellow, Furax, and we have got the better of him, in spite of his writ and levy. I found so many flaws to be picked in his proceedings, that he was frightened at his own temerity, and was glad to take half the sum owing him, in cash, and turn over his claim and suit to me. I shall thus control the first judgment against your property and the levy on your furniture, which it is a capital good thing to have. This was all done last night, and well done. Mind, I did not take it to myself, and I have made a condition that any proceedings shall be in the name of Furax."

"But if you paid half the debt, where did you find the money. I had none and—"

"Oh, I had a few thousand idle sestertia and they may as well be used in this way as in any other, and better. Besides, don't you see I am your first judgment creditor, ahead of every one else, and what better security can I have?"

"Very well," said the Prince, "I thank you, most sincerely, for this and all your kindness, but, Vindex, what did you mean by there being provision for the Princess?"

"I mean just this. All your lands are entirely free of debt, thank fortune, and being clear, your wife has a right of dower in them, worth enough to provide for her handsomely. Assignatus, to whom you conveyed them, yesterday, in trust for your creditors, cannot make sale of a square inch of them, because no one would take the title without a release of her dower right by the Princess, and for that the creditors must pay her its full value."

"I always supposed," said the Prince, "that a wife's right of dower was something she did not come into till her husband died. I can see that if I died it would be worth a good deal, but I am not dead yet, though this trouble may kill me very soon."

"It will help to keep you alive" said the old jurisconsult, "because it will give a new train to your

thoughts, and a new impulse to your activities.
Now about the right of dower. That is perfectly
plain. The moment the wedding ring is on the
wife's finger, and the knot tied, she is endowed of all
her husband's lands. This is a property right, which
she cannot be deprived of, without her own consent,
so long as she continues his wife. In case of his
death, the right becomes absolute, and then she is
entitled to one-third, for life, of the rents of the lands
or, if she choose, she may have one-third of the
lands set off to her, under the direction of the court,
and hold them as long as she lives. This is what
we call 'admeasuring' her dower. While the husband is living, of course, the wife's right of dower is
contingent—'inchoate,'—as the law calls it."

"Why not call it something a little more unintel-
ligible?" said the Prince. "The jargon of the law is
the strangest thing imaginable. I believe it is part
of your stock in trade."

"Of course it is ; what would any science be without its technical nomenclature. 'Inchoate' means
primarily, in a chaotic state, and nothing can be more
without form or fixed conditions than a wife's dower
right, as long as her husband is living, and nobody
can foretell which of the two will outlive the other."

"How then can such a right have any value? It
must be mere guess work."

"It is. And so the law guesses at it, and has
adopted a table of values of the contingent right,
according to the age of the wife."

"Then, when I signed the parchment, yesterday,

Assignatus did not get a clear title for the benefit of the creditors. It was subject to this contingent right, as you call it, of the Princess."

" Just so and rightfully, because, although contingent, it is property, and she must be paid for it. Your case is very unusual. Ordinarily a man mortgages his lands, if he has any, before he fails, and his wife joins in the mortgage and releases her dower. But your lands are clear of debt and the dower right is intact. The creditors understand this and have already made overtures to pay ; in fact, I think that we can get between fifty thousand and one hundred thousand sestertia for it. They must pay more than the value by the tables, because they cannot compel a release."

The Prince was silent for a few minutes. At last he said,

" Vindex, I do not believe the Princess will take the money."

" Why not ? "

" Because she will think it is not right. She will be very firm in the idea that everything must go to the creditors."

" Certainly, everything the law gives them. The law does not give them the dower right. It belongs to her."

" She will give them this besides," said the Prince.

" Then she will be a very foolish woman," said Vindex, " and she will simply throw away her property, at the very moment when she needs it most.

The dower right is hers, and she should make it
worth what it will bring."

"You must talk this matter over with the
Princess, yourself," said the Prince, " if you will wait,
I will send her to you, only I know very well how
it will end. The dower right will go to the creditors."

The Princess and Prima, while washing the breakfast things, with their own hands, were discussing
plans for the future; a small house, in the upper part
of the island whereon the Imperial City was built,
stood on the lands belonging to the Prince, and was
available for the immediate occupation of the
family. The Princess was determined to quit the
palace, at once, and preparations for the removal
were, already, in progress. Fortunately, she had
pursued a system of unusual economy for some
months; the bad name given to her by Domesticus
had made a kind of enforced interregnum in the
household service, and old Patella had been the
main-stay of the family. The Prince had been dis-
inclined to having any company in the house, and
everything having favored retrenchment, the
Princess had been able to put by, out of the ample
provision the Prince always made for current wants,
a considerable sum, sufficient for all present needs.
As she was never in debt to any one, she was free
from obligations, and her savings came in opportunely in the present distress.

She came, at the call of the Prince, and he left
her alone with the old jurisconsult. He could
hardly tell why, but he did not care to be present

at the interview, and he thought he knew how it would end.

The wily advocate was as shrewd in his sympathies as he was in the more ordinary and active duties of his calling. He saw, at once, that the little lady expected and desired no condolence, or tear-drops ; and after the customary salutations, he purposely began, in a blunt way,—

"I hear you intend quitting these premises at once."

"As soon as possible," said the Princess. "I suppose we are in no danger of being turned out, for a day or two."

"You can stay just as long as you choose. It is out of the question to rent a palace like this, at the present time. The summer, which is just at hand, is the wrong season. A bill may be posted in front, but until a tenant is found, it is better you should remain in possession, and care for the property. Besides, an occupied house always rents better than a vacant one."

"I prefer to go," said the Princess. "Our old servant, Patella, will care for everything, and we shall avoid the expense of keeping up a large establishment. And if it cannot be leased, perhaps it can be sold."

"No," said Vindex, seizing the first opportunity of introducing the subject he wanted to discuss. "Neither the palace, nor any of the Prince's lands can be sold, as yet, so as to give a clear title, and no one will buy them without a clear title."

12

"Why not?" asked the Princess, in some alarm. "Has he not a good title? Surely he came by them all honestly."

"Yes, a good title, but I said a *clear* title. You have a right of dower in all the Prince's lands. It is a charge upon them, and without your release of that dower right, the title is not marketable. No one wants to buy property with a right of dower outstanding."

"I suppose," said the Princess, "that is why I have had to sign the parchment whenever the Prince sold any land, and say 'yes,' to something a young man would mumble over to me, after I signed."

"Yes, that is just the reason, and whenever you joined with your husband in signing, that act cut off your right of dower, but none of these lands have been sold, and so your dower right remains your property, and the creditors will pay you a good round sum to release it."

"But I never was paid a round sum, or a square sum, or any kind of a sum, when I used to sign with the Prince."

"That was because he got the purchase money, and you got your share, in support and mainte-nance, for which the Prince paid, but now he gets nothing; he simply transfers his property to pay his debts, and so you ought to be paid for your release of dower."

"Who is to pay me?"

"The person to whom the Prince conveyed all

his properties yesterday, for the equal benefit of all his creditors."

" Who is that person ? "

" Assignatus, I presume you know him."

" I know him very well," said the Princess. " He was married the same week with the Prince and myself. His eldest daughter is just two days older than Prima, no, let me see, Prima is two days older than she—well, I am not quite sure which it is."

" Anyway," said Vindex, " he is an excellent man, and the creditors have perfect confidence in him. All that remains is for them to fix the sum they are willing to pay you, and for you to agree to it. The amount will be at least fifty thousand sestertia ; they will furnish this to Assignatus, and he will pay you, and it will make a good provision for your wants."

" Why cannot I have it in land," said the Princess. " I remember now, since you began to speak about this, that the Princess Vidua had a house given her, and she told me it was admeasured to her for dower. It was over twenty-five feet front, and had land on both sides of it. I suppose that is why they measured it."

" That was different. Her husband was dead. The wife gets none of the land, or the rents, until after the husband's death."

" Then has the Prince got to die, before this right is of any value ? Is all this on the idea that he is going to die ? It is perfectly dreadful ! I don't want to talk about it, or think about it. It is positively cruel ! "

" You don't quite understand," said Vindex, " the wife does not, to be sure, come into the full enjoyment of her dower right till her husband dies—"

" But I could not enjoy anything, if the Prince were to die—why do you talk to me in this way ? Isn't it bad enough for my poor husband to fail, without calculating on his death ? Indeed I do not understand it at all, and I don't want to understand it, if this is what it means."

" My dear lady," said Vindex—who, perceiving that the flood-gates of feeling were in danger of giving way, and of all reason and common sense being swept out of reach and sight, paused for a moment, and then resumed on a new basis,—" I am delighted to see the Prince looking as well as he does this morning, and I am sure, before long, he will see many things to encourage him. He is not likely to suffer in health, or in spirits, permanently, and what I am suggesting to you has no reference whatever to his death. It is simply a matter of business, and I will not trouble you any further with it, if it is distasteful to you. I had not finished explaining what it really was."

" Pardon me," said the Princess, " if I interrupted you ; I will promise to listen ; only you frightened me dreadfully in saying what you did. Now, go on, please."

" What I wanted to say was that you have and own, at the present time, a right of dower in all the lands of the Prince. The law of the land gives it to you. It is yours, and no one's else. It is worth a

large sum of money. Your husband has transferred
the lands to Assignatus, as a trustee, for the benefit of
his creditors. They are still subject to your dower
right, as a charge, because you did not join in the
deed to Assignatus, and unless the creditors can
have that charge removed, by procuring a release
of your dower right, from yourself, to the trustee,
they cannot sell the lands free and clear of it.
Therefore, they want to pay you a sum of money
and have you release your right, in consideration
of that payment."

"I think I understand it now," said the Princess.
"If the mumbling young man had come here, yesterday, and brought the parchment, by which the
Prince transferred the lands to Assignatus, and I
had signed it, and said, 'yes', when he said whatever it is he says, then my dower right would have
been gone. Because I did not sign and say 'yes,'
I own it still, and the creditors want me to sign a
separate parchment, all by myself, to make it just the
same as if I had signed, yesterday, with the Prince."

"That is precisely the case; you have put it as
clearly as possible," said Vindex, delighted to see
that the flood-gates were sound and tight, and that
reason and good sense were not swept away.

"Then this dower right is mine, to keep or sell
as I please?"

"Unquestionably."

"And the money the creditors are willing to pay
for it will be in my hand, to do what I please with?"

"Certainly."

"And when the creditors get the separate parchment from me, they will have all that the Prince, or I, or both of us, together, could possibly give them."

"That is so."

"Then please prepare the parchment and send the young man, and I will sign it, and say ' yes ', and there will be an end. I will have none of their money."

" But my dear Princess ! "

"Why should I ? If I had the price, in my hand, I should pay it all back to them. If I had a million sestertia, I would give them, every one, to the Prince, to help pay his just debts. Why should I not do, to-day, what I would have done, yesterday, without a word of question, or a thought of pay? It is quite too late for me to be setting a price for signing my name."

" But," said Vindex, "you were never in this plight before. It was all right for you to sign off, without any price, so long as your husband was selling the land in the ordinary course of dealing. Now, since he has failed, it is very different."

"Am I to be better off because he has failed ? " asked the Princess. "It seems a very strange thing that when a man fails, the first thing his creditors must do is to pay his wife a great sum of money."

" No, you are not to be a bit better off. Before the failure you had this property, and you have it now, but the creditors are not your creditors, and they have to deal with you separately ; before the

failure there was, in effect, no separation of your
interest from your husband's."

" Then, instead of drawing us closer together, the
failure is going to separate us," said the Princess.
" Never, with my consent! We have always been
one in prosperity, and we shall cling to one another
in adversity, and, I hope, always."

The flood-gates were loosening again and the
veteran practitioner began to fear that they would
certainly burst open, with ruinous consequences.
He tried another tack.

"You would prefer, then, not to receive anything
from the creditors for a release of your dower
right ? "

" I will not take a single sestertium from them;
not one."

"And of course," said the wily old advocate, "you
would not like to acknowledge having received any
sum, however small, from them ? "

"Of course not," said the Little Lady, walking
into the trap he laid for her, as innocently as ever a
fly was enticed into a spider's web.

"Then," said he, "you cannot possibly make the
dower right over to them, because the transfer would
not be good unless they paid something for it, or, at
least, you acknowledged having received something."

"Why not? I recollect when the Prince gave a
house and some land, in the country, to his sister,
she paid nothing, not the smallest sum, he told me
so, and I signed too."

"Yes, because there the consideration was natural love and affection, but that only applies between relations, and besides, it is quite inconceivable, and wholly unknown to the law, that any one should entertain natural love and affection for his creditors."

The Little Lady thought she had natural love and affection enough for the whole world, but to love her husband's creditors as herself was something of a strain, even upon the most amiable disposition, and when she found that the consideration of natural love and affection could only apply between kindred, she was brought to a point where she saw she had been too sweeping in her declaration that she would not even acknowledge the receipt of one sestertium, in exchange for her dower right.

This was all that Vindex wanted, for the moment. He was too wise to provoke further controversy with the Princess, and as he wished to gain time, he preferred to retreat from the contest, in good order, under cover of the obscurity he had succeeded in throwing over the matter, on the question of consideration.

The Princess was a little nonplussed, and the subject was dropped, apparently because neither party to the conversation was in a position to press the point on which they had respectively been persistent.

"I want to ask you about the furniture," said the Princess. "Ought it not to be sold next Fall? It will bring so much better prices then."

Vindex had his own secret intentions about the

furniture, which he meant to carry out, for the benefit of the Princess, at all hazards. He had planned
and determined that she should never leave the
palace; that her dower right should provide all
present means of support; that the furniture should
all be hers, in a way he meant to work out; and that,
in the end, the Prince's debts should be compro-
mised and here-in stated, if not in his fortune, at least
in a competency. He had found himself blocked
by the Princess, first, in her resolve to vacate the
palace, next, by her refusal to receive the value of
her dower right, and, now, she was suggesting
something which would be fatal to his hidden plans
on her behalf, in the matter of the furniture. But
here he felt he was master of the situation, and he
meant to carry things with a high hand.

"The furniture may have to be sold, under execution, very soon—under the first judgment and levy."

"But that will sacrifice it. It ought to bring a
very large sum. It is just as good as new, all of it.
It has had the very best care; then there are all the
pictures, and statues, and vases, and ornaments—
they will surely sell best in the Fall."

"Images and gimcracks don't bring half their
value, at any time," said Vindex, "and as to old furniture, it is a drug in the market."

"Images, gimcracks, and old furniture!" Was
this all that the eye of the law could discern in the
treasures with which the palace of the Prince was
stored?

The Little Lady was as indignant as Vindex

meant she should be at his brutal words. He well
knew that, next to the ties of nature, the attachment
of the female heart to the furniture around which
the associations of home and family have clustered,
is something which will cling to its object, like the
carving to a four-post bedstead. He felt for her,
but he was determined he would not be out-gener-
aled, this time, and his plan was a pet one, of his own
special devising, which he was bent on pursuing.

The Little Lady's wrath was great, but her lovely
temper checked its rising waves. She said, with
evident feeling and some dignity,

"You will pardon me for putting a higher value
than perhaps it deserves, on this part of the Prince's
property. My only wish is to have it go, as far as
may be, toward paying his debts. And pardon me
again, but I thought you said there was no necessity for our leaving the house, and if this is so, why
is there any fear of an immediate sale?"

"But you say you will not remain in the house;
and if you quit, the judgment creditor may come
and sell the furniture, at any time. He would very
likely wait, if you did not leave." It occurred to
Vindex that here was a string he might pull so as
to detain the Princess in the palace. But he was at
fault, for she replied, promptly;—

"No, that cannot be; but why not induce the first
judgment creditor to wait, all the same; he will get
more by doing so. Who did you say he was?

"He is,—that is, he was—yes,—the name of the
creditor in the judgment is Furax, a very vindictive,

grasping, difficult man to deal with ; a kind of man you would never want to meet, or know anything about, or be under any obligation to."

"But surely you could induce him to delay, when there is no object in his pushing matters."

"I don't think I have the slightest influence over him," said Vindex, who was now a great deal more anxious to end this interview with the Princess than he had been to begin it. "You must prepare for the worst in this matter, but, in the end, all will come right, and now I must be going ; excuse my detaining you so long, and kindly inform the Prince that I am leaving, as I want a word with him before I go."

The Princess knew that a professional man must not be detained, and she was, herself, willing to have a respite for reflection. As she left the room, the Prince, who was in an adjoining apartment, entered, and the moment he was alone with Vindex, he asked,

"What success ? Will the Princess accept anything for her dower right ?"

"She does not want to. Woman-like, she has put herself on a ground that does more credit to her heart than her head. Fortunately, we are to have a breathing spell, and I have some ideas out of which good may come, without going counter to her views. But, my dear Prince, you must promise me one thing, and keep your promise, as you hope for help in your need. Do not, for the world, let the Princess know that I control, or have anything to do with the judgment of Furax. This is absolutely essential for her good, which, you know, I have close at heart. As I told you, the claim was not transferred to my name, and so you do not know who owns it. She must not suspect that I have the least interest in it. Give me your word on that."

"I think you are entitled to claim this of me," said the Prince, "so I promise as you ask."

"Very good," said the jurisconsult, and he went his way to his clients.

# CHAPTER XVIII.

## LEAVING HOME.

THE Little Lady looked back on her interview with the sagacious Vindex with a sense of discomfort. In spite of his lucid explanation of the law of dower, and her clear comprehension of it at the time, she found some difficulty, in the retrospect, in keeping the matter clearly before her mind. She appealed to the Prince for a solution of her doubts, and they discussed the whole subject, according to the light they had, which, being all borrowed from the instructions they had received separately from the same source, was serviceable only so far as its reflected rays were coincident.

"I cannot see," said the Princess, "how Vindex could expect to make me believe that your creditors would pay me a large sum of money for something I have not got, and may never have, and that I never expect to have; because you know, dearest, I want to die first—and I know I shall. He says it is property; but I cannot divine how a thing is property one hasn't got. My linen, and my camel's hair shawl, and my laces, and the jewelry you have given me, are mine, and I will go to prison before I will give them up, because your creditors have

189

nothing to do with them. Why, there is my mother's silver tea-service, marked with my name, which, if Prima should marry and have a daughter, and she should be named for me, would belong to her, right off, to be hers when I die; that is what I call property. But how can you own a thing when it is all guess-work whether you will live long enough to have it?"

"As I understand it," said the Prince, "it is the contingency that is valued, on the doctrine of chances."

"Then it is nothing more nor less than a lottery," said the Princess; "it is dealing in a chance, and a chance in your own husband's life. I felt it was something dreadful all the time. How these juris-consults, as they call themselves, can twist and turn things! I thought all lotteries were prohibited by law."

"I suppose," said the Prince, "that what the law allows can hardly be illegal. Vindex says the court has tables which fix the value. Now, if your contingent dower right is something which the law recognizes, and if it lies on the land, like a mortgage, and the creditors want to lift it off, and are willing to pay to get rid of it, I should say it was all right for them to offer and for you to take the money."

"It may be perfectly right, as you say," said the Princess, "for them to offer to pay, but I cannot feel that it would be right for me to take their money and keep it. If I were to pick up so much money in the street, even if the law said I could have it, I should want to find the owner, for all that; and if I couldn't find the owner, and had to keep it, I should want to give it to you, to help pay your debts. One thing is certain, Vindex may be a great jurist on dower rights and contingencies, but he knows nothing about furniture or pictures, and I am afraid he is a very heartless man."

"He is as good and true a friend as we have in the world," said the Prince. "I dare say he is not very well posted in upholstery or the fine arts. He is an old bachelor and belongs to the kind that is satisfied with the mahogany and hair-cloth of a past generation."

"But think of his being willing to have all the furniture in this house sold in mid-summer! It will be thrown away. What ought the things, all taken together, to bring? I will go to work with Prima, to-morrow morning, and make a complete list of everything, with prices, and send it to Vindex. It may open his old eyes to their value. Why, the set in our bedroom alone ought to bring nearly as much as it cost; it ought to go very high."

"If it could be sold by weight, it would," said the Prince. "It weighs several tons."

"It is all splendid solid rosewood," said the Princess, "just as different as possible from the glued-together, flimsy things they make nowadays. I hate waste. If Vindex does not prevent this sale taking place at this season, he is no friend of mine. And who is this Furax whom he says is so fierce? Do you know him?"

"Only by name. He is a man who buys notes

and drafts, and he had some of ours. You had much better leave all this entirely to Vindex. If the furniture should bring all it cost, it would be only a drop in the bucket, just now. Vindex will take care of everything."

"I am almost afraid of him," said the Princess. "No, I am not afraid of anybody, so long as I am doing right, not even of Furax; and if need be, I will find him out and get him to postpone the sale, and save the furniture from sacrifice."

This was an alarming suggestion, and the Prince made haste to change the subject, inwardly resolving to acquaint Vindex, at the earliest moment, with the apprehensions and the intentions of the Princess.

In the meantime, the preparations for the exodus from the palace went on apace. In a few days the Princess was ready to leave with all the articles which she determined, after deciding every doubtful case against herself, she had a right to carry away with her, as her special property, or that of her children. The long list of the furniture and other things, she prepared with Prima's aid, and dispatched to Vindex, according to the declaration made to the Prince, and by him communicated to the old jurisconsult, who, somewhat to the Prince's surprise, said it was just what he wanted to have.

When the morning arrived which the Princess had fixed for her departure, after giving some final instructions to Patella, as she sat by herself in the room she had so long loved to call her own, and felt, more than anything else, a kind of surprise at her own courage in the moment of bidding it farewell, Prima came in and said that the old servant was outside and desired to speak to her for a moment.

"What does Patella want, Prima? I spent an hour with her after breakfast, down stairs, giving her all the directions about everything."

"Yes, but since then she has dressed herself and gone out, and now she has come back, and says she has a great favor to ask of you."

"I hardly know what favors I am able to bestow on any one just now, but let Patella come in."

The door was opened, and the old woman entered with a quick step, for she was light of foot in spite of her years, and wiry of frame. But as she came nearer the Princess, she stopped, as if the courage she had mustered up for her errand was almost failing her; then, with a sudden plunge of her right hand into the depths of a pocket in her dress, she brought forth a leathern pouch, tied with a stout string, out of which she drew a roll of bills of the currency of the realm, and, with an almost convulsive movement, cast it into the lap of the Princess.

"Please, my lady," said Patella, "I have gone and got my money, and it is you I want to have it. I am poor, and do not want it, but a rich lady, like yourself has always been, cannot live without money all the time. It is a thousand sestertia, and I know very well it will all come back to me when I need it."

The Little Lady had borne up against everything.

13

She had met the sharp shock of the failure without flinching. She had spurned the proffered purchase of her dower right, almost with disdain. She had not quailed before the vindictiveness of Furax. She had nerved herself to quit house and home with courage, and even with cheerfulness, but at this soft touch of loving-kindness from a humble heart and hand, she gave way completely, and broke into a flood of tears and convulsive sobs.

Patella was frightened at this unexpected and unusual outburst of feeling. She was on her knees, in an instant, clasping the hands of her mistress, which she kissed with all the fervor that had impelled her generous gift.

Prima, who thought she had never seen anything more pathetic, looked on with moist eyes.

The Princess recovered herself in a few moments. In the brief interval of unrestrained feeling, she had not only gained a needed relief from the over-strain to which she had been subjected, but also found courage for the only response worthy of the generous self-sacrifice of which Patella's proffered gift was the perfect fruit.

"I thank you from the bottom of my heart, Patella. I will take the money, gratefully, and you may be sure I will return it; but your kindness is something that touches me most deeply, and this is a debt I fear I shall find it hard to repay."

The old woman went away happier than she had ever been in her life, for she had dreaded a repulse, or, at least, a refusal.

When she was alone with her mother, Prima was the first to speak.

" I am so glad you took the money. Of course, I know it will not be wanted or used, but it would have broken her heart if you had refused it."

" No money was ever safer than this," said the Princess, tightening her clasp on the roll of bills, " and certainly none was ever more lovingly lent. It is a good omen, and I accept it. Deliverance from these evil days is not far distant; but how strange that the first note of succor should have come from the ranks of Domesticus!"

# CHAPTER XIX.

## AT A GREAT SACRIFICE.

"PRIMA TO JUVENTUS. . . . Our new home is pleasant, not by contrast with the one we have left, but in itself. I will tell you how to find it when you come hither. Take the old broad roadway, northward beyond the central campus, on the sunset side, until you come to a lane, striking off toward the river bank, which you will know by a round stone tower at its corner, and, following this lane a few rods, you come, on the right hand side, to a square white house of the oldest fashion, on a little bluff, with two willows overhanging the gate. The house is a relic of the past, left almost alone. The last tenant moved away in the spring to a new home, so that our coming works harm to no one. I like the wide outlook which takes in river, shores, and sky. It reminds me of what the dear old painter-poet who went—

> 'Piping down the valleys wild,
> Piping songs of pleasant glee,'

wrote to his 'archangel sculptor' friend about his little cottage by the sea: 'Heaven opens here on all sides her golden gates; her windows are not obstructed by vapors.'

196

"All are pleased, save Stella. With her, we have had no end of trouble. The removal from the Via Quinta was a great blow, as it separated her from a choice circle of admirers. In the midst of our hard work of settling here, she must needs go off on a picnic which, off course, provoked the most violent tempest and tornado of the season, and the consequence was that she took to her bed for a fortnight. Mamma and I nursed her through the sickness, or, rather, Mamma did, and I helped a little. She was disappointed at not having one or two leading physicians called in, and I think, at one time, began to be apprehensive she might die without the faintest prospect of a Wake. As soon as she got well, she went away for good, without a word of thanks, simply a good-bye, and we hear, through Patella, she has made a bad marriage. I thought her awfully ungrateful, but Mamma says we must not misjudge, and what seems ingratitude in these people is often only a dread of appearing to be under an obligation, and she still thinks there are some stray virtues hidden under all Stella's perverseness.

" Papa's affairs are improving. The old jurisconsult Vindex has them in charge. He insists upon it there was no need of our quitting the palace, but Mamma says it was indispensable, and I think she is right."

The better aspect of the Prince's affairs alluded to in the above extract from Prima's letter was a cheering fact.

Vindex had entered, with all his energies, upon the task of extricating his old friend and client from the ruin so suddenly precipitated. He was, at first, considerably provoked by the headlong haste with which the Princess had insisted upon leaving the palace; and he was also not a little taken aback by her positive refusal to accept the proffered payment for her dower right. While he condemned her want of judgment, he could not help admiring the feeling from which her false conclusions flowed. Nevertheless, he was fully determined that no illusive sentiment, however pure and praiseworthy its source, should stand in the way of those absolute and paramount legal rights to which his moral as well as his intellectual vision was adjusted.

He saw how he could turn the strangely illogical resolve of the Princess to account, for her own ultimate good, and he lost no time in calling the creditors together, and stating to them, with the most ingenuous frankness, the decision she had made to decline their offer for her dower right, on the ground that everything should belong to the creditors, which either she or her husband could make over to them.

This was a bold stroke. Vindex had found, by long experience, that there is no force in human affairs so potent as the plain truth. "The truth," he was accustomed to say, "is always your best hold. Honest men will believe all you tell them. Dishonest men will believe nothing. Thus the truth will serve you, with the one class, as an open door through which your minds can freely meet, and

with the other class, as a closed screen behind which
you may find it convenient to hide." So it proved
in this instance. The guileless among the creditors
were in accord in commending the action of the
Princess, to such a degree that they brought themselves to the point of hesitation, if not unwilling-
ness, to take advantage of her rare magnanimity,
and unitedly disclaimed any disposition to be unjust
to her, even at her own request. The few trickish
traders among the body thought this show of
disinterestedness a pretence contrived by the artful
Vindex to ensnare them to their disadvantage.
They were in the dark as to what his crooked design
might be, and so they were afraid to act; and the
majority being, as is usually the case, honest and
fair-minded men, it was finally agreed that the
whole matter should be deferred until the lands
could be sold to advantage.

Vindex thus gained time, always the best ally of
defendants and debtors, and besides, gained the
good-will of the leading creditors, and their active
sympathies on the side of the Princess, in voting
down the minority of distrusting malcontents.

Having thus neutralized, and even utilized, the
mistaken action of the Princess, without coming
into collision with her views or wishes, Vindex
went on to put into due course of execution his deep-
laid plan for securing the furniture of the palace
for her benefit, before she could circumvent him by
any more troublesome displays of honest activity
against her own interests.

He gave orders to enforce the levy which, as we
have seen, had been made at the instance of Furax,
the hostile creditor, who was the earliest in the field
against the unfortunate Prince, whose swift action
had placed him ahead of all the others, and whose
rights had been purchased by Vindex, and were now
enforceable as he pleased.   Accordingly, it was duly
heralded and proclaimed that the household furniture, pictures, and other works of art, and all the
contents of the palace, would be sold at public outcry on the premises on the seventh day after the first
heralding.

This hostile action was taken in the name of
Furax, according to the arrangement made by
Vindex when he bought the claim.   When it came
to the Little Lady's ears it did not surprise her at
all.   She did not believe Vindex had done a thing
to stop the sale, and she wondered, more than ever,
why the Prince left everything in the hands of this
old, and, as she thought, slow-going veteran, instead
of employing some young and enterprising jurisconsult, who would find some way, by hook or by
crook, to trip up Furax, and delay the sale, for she
was so convinced of the wrong involved in hastening
it, that she was almost ready to see every law, divine
and human, set aside, temporarily, in order to accomplish this just end.

The Prince seemed to her strangely indifferent
to the subject, and as he persisted in refusing to interfere with Vindex, the Princess again declared her
intention of going in person to Furax, to satisfy

him, as she was quite certain she could, that the furniture would be sacrificed, to his great disadvantage and loss. It required all the authority and expostulation the Prince could bring to bear to convince her that this would be a breach of dignity and decorum which could not be allowed. She finally yielded to his views, but could not forbear a thrust at Vindex, in the remark that it was passing strange to her that people thought so much of him, when, with all his supposed skill and learning, he could not get a furniture sale postponed for a few weeks in mid-summer.

The Prince turned the matter off as lightly as he could. He tried to convince the Princess that it was not of any vital consequence, at the risk, which he well knew he took, of being regarded as almost as cold-blooded and heartless as Vindex himself. The Princess well knew that she could not expect from him, or any of his unfeeling sex, the full sympathy she needed on this sore subject, or a comprehension of feelings they could not share; and she excused the Prince because he was now absorbed in new engagements which were a part of the improved state of things to which Prima had alluded. His good standing and repute, his long experience in affairs, and his mature abilities, had opened for him several opportunities of activity in new fields of enterprise, and everything seemed conspiring toward a better outcome from his troubles than he had at first thought possible. At all events, present wants, on a moderate scale of living, were sure to be supplied, and this was a great relief.

The Little Lady kept silence, and waited until the morning of the sale arrived; then, after the Prince had gone for the day, she said to Prima,

"I must go to the palace, and I want you to go with me; I cannot endure the thought of all those things being sold off, without knowing anything about it. Everything will be carted away to-morrow and that will be the end." And her eyes filled with tears.

"But people will see us there," said Prima.

"Every one we know is in the country. We can double our veils and not be recognized, and Patella can arrange a screen, or something, so that we need not be noticed."

Prima gave way as she saw that the consequences of checking her mother's feeling and purpose might be perilous; and on reflection she saw nothing very hazardous in the proposal.

The trip to the Via Quinta was easily made by the public conveyance which passed near the house, and they soon found themselves within the portals of the palace, made conspicuous by the red flag which was the conventional signal of a public sale in the Imperial City. "To this complexion has it come at last," thought Prima, as she looked sadly at its vengeful color, fluttering over the threshold of her lost home.

With the ready aid of Patella, they placed themselves behind some of the taller pieces of furniture which had been placed in prominence on the main floor of the palace, so that they could see and hear what was going on, without being subjected to unpleasant scrutiny.

The Little Lady's judgment as to the ill-advised time of the sale was borne out by the character of the attendance it had invited. The throng which invaded the precincts of the palace gave little indication of furnishing appreciative or liberal bidders. The class of customers for the high grade of articles to be put up for forced sale was wholly unrepresented. The great majority were evidently drawn to the palace by idle curiosity, and, with the exception of a few who might be supposed to belong to the fraternity of dealers in second-hand furniture, and only bought at great bargains, there was no one who looked like a probable purchaser.

In striking contrast with the generally commonplace and uninteresting air of the assemblage, was the dignified figure of Vindex, who was one of the earliest comers, and who was attended by a subservient assistant intent on watching every glance and gesture of his superior.

The outcrier, whose business it was to conduct the sale, announced, after the distribution of the lists, that it would begin on the lowest, or underground, floor of the palace, that it would then be continued on the topmost floor, after which he would come down stairs, selling the articles on each lower floor, in successive order.

This announcement had no sooner been made,

than an aggressive-looking individual, who had been engaged in inspecting the various articles displayed in the grand apartments on the main floor, marking prices on the list, and testing the upholstery by sitting down consecutively on all the chairs and sofas, called out, in a loud tone :—

"This is a very queer way of conducting a sale! Why don't you start by selling the things we have come here to buy, instead of going underground, to begin with pots and kettles?"

The outcrier of the Imperial City was always ready for every questioner, either with the hard answer which provoketh wrath, or the soft answer which turneth it away. This time it was the soft answer which was forthcoming.

"Certainly, by all means; we want everybody to be suited. If there is any article on this floor which any person present wants to have put up and sold immediately, before going down stairs, we will put it up; and everything put up will be sold to the highest bidder."

Nothing could be fairer than this, and attention was turned to the aggressive individual, who was evidently disappointed that his complaint had been so promptly and fully met, and that he had been summarily deprived of a grievance; but he responded to the unexpected invitation :

"Put up the clock and candelabra on the mantel over there. I suppose the clock is warranted to keep good time."

"The clock and candelabra are put up," said the

outcrier; "I will warrant the clock to go ahead of any clock of its description in this city; that may make it a little too fast for you; but any article that doesn't suit may be returned and the money will be refunded. Now what shall I have for the clock and candelabra?"

"They cost three hundred sestertia," said the Princess, in a whisper, to Prima; "we bought them years ago—Secundus was a baby. The clock never went too fast; it lost a little sometimes, but not much."

"What shall I have," repeated the outcrier, "for this superb lot—clock and candelabra?"

"Fifteen sestertia," said the aggressive individual. There was a faint shriek. It came from the Princess, who could not resist the temptation of stepping from her hiding-place as the bidding began, and to whom the idea of associating her best clock and candelabra with this pitiful sum was a shock too great to endure in silence.

Her involuntary exclamation had the immediate effect of turning upon her a large number of eyes, including the particularly sharp pair which were the special property of Vindex. To him she had betrayed herself, but only to him, and he made no sign of recognition. The outcrier wilfully and maliciously, as it seemed to her, interpreted her little shriek as a bid, according to the custom of his craft, and putting it at his own figure, went on,—

"Twenty-five sestertia is bid by the lady in the veil—only twenty-five: make it thirty-five?" And he

turned from the dismayed Princess to the aggressive
individual, who, greatly to her relief, made it thirty-
five, and the outcrier took up the refrain,

"Thirty-five,—only thirty-five, Madam,—will you
say forty?"

Before the Princess could settle, in her distracted
thoughts, whether keeping perfectly still, or shaking
her head wildly, or rushing from the place, was the
most effectual way of escaping the responsibilites
of a supposed bidder, the attendant of Vindex
called out, in a sharp tone—

"Two hundred sestertia."

"Two hundred—two hundred," said the outcrier,
accepting the new bid with the nonchalance he had
been cultivating for a quarter of a century. "Shall
I have more? Two hundred sestertia is bid."

"Prima," whispered the Princess, "this is wonderful. It is the very figure I put on my list. Why
if everything sells at this rate, it will be perfectly
splendid. What a good-looking man that is who
bid. He is standing close by Vindex."

"I rather think he is doing the bidding of Vindex,
in a double sense," said Prima, beginning to be
puzzled at what was going on; but the Princess was
too much occupied in watching the proceedings to
notice her remark.

No one competed with the last bidder; the clock
and candelabra were knocked down to him; his
name was called for, and promptly given as Ignotus;
the purchase was recorded, and thereupon the
outcrier, in his blandest manner, inquired of the

aggressive individual if there was anything else on that floor worth two hundred sestertia which he would like to start at fifteen?  On this there was a general laugh by the entire company, with such irritating effect on the individual that with some unpremeditated but forcible expressions of disgust, he made a rapid exit from the palace.

" I am so glad he has gone," said the Princess to Prima.  "To think of his trying to get those things for fifteen sestertia!  He cannot be an honest man. It would have been no better than stealing."

No further objection being interposed to the order of sale indicated at the beginning by the out-crier, everybody descended, in good humor, to the lower parts of the house, the Princess being now thoroughly aroused by the auspicious episode of the first bidding, and Prima being very curious to watch the progress of events, which she suspected was being shaped by Vindex.

The first lot put up for sale, below stairs, was a collection of old pails and saucepans, which the Princess told Prima were not worth, all together, more than a single sestertium.  But no sooner were they offered for sale, and before an ancient boarding-house keeper who had come, in her best outfit, to bid especially for these articles, had the opportunity of saying a word, Ignotus bid two sestertia, and they were knocked down to him, no one competing; and so on, as each succeeding lot was exposed, he promptly offered twice its possible value, and be-came the purchaser, to the great amazement of the

disinterested spectators, the consternation of the
intending bidders, and the mute wonder of the Princess and Prima.

By the time the list of the down-stairs articles had
been gone through, the entire property in that part
of the premises, which would have been dear at two
hundred and fifty sestertia, had been sold for five
hundred. It began to be apparent to the whole
company that there was no chance for any one to
compete with such a bidder as Ignotus, whose
readiness to part with his money seemed a conclu-
sive indication that he had parted with his senses at
some prior period, and whose determination to buy
everything, at twice its value, made it a waste of
time for any one else to assist further at such a
farcical performance. The professional dealers, seeing that there were no bargains to be hoped for, did
not care to mount to the top story, and took themselves off; and as to the small remnant of the company who made the long ascent to the upper
regions, it seemed to the Princess, as she surveyed
them, that they were all mere lookers-on at the
reckless prodigality of Ignotus.

The outcry was recommenced; and again he bid
off everything, as fast as it was set up for sale. Old
bedsteads, tables, chairs, and washstands, hardly
worth carting away, were struck off to him at
prices for which they could have been replaced
twice over by brand-new articles of the same description. He made a clean sweep, giving no one
else a chance for so much as a soap-dish or a slop-

pail; and by the time the descent to the third story
was made, the effect of his selfish monopoly of pur-
chasing had been to drive every one from the sale,
except a mere handful of idlers, in whom the expe-
rienced eye of the outcrier discerned only the un-
mistakable non-bidders who hang about salesrooms
with no ability or intention to buy.

At this stage, and with as much formality as if
the original crowd before which the outcry was
begun were still present, he announced that if any
person desired any particular article on the third
floor, or elsewhere in the palace, to be separately set
up, it should be done; if not, he was instructed to
say that the whole remaining contents of the palace, as set forth in the list, would be now put up
as one lot, and sold together. The small cluster of
people who had remained, solely for further partici-
pation in what seemed to them the good joke of
Ignotus wasting his money, had no possible concern in opposing any method of sale which seemed
good to the outcrier, and they made no response to
his inquiry, whereupon he immediately put up, in a
single lot, everything in the palace which had not
been previously sold.

Ignotus, with customary promptness, bid five
hundred sestertia.

Dead silence followed for a moment, broken by a
sharp cry from the Princess.

"Five hundred sestertia! Why they are worth
fifteen thousand!"

"Do I hear fifteen thousand?" said the outcrier,

14

turning his swift professional glance on the Princess. " Fifteen thousand,—shall I have more ? Make it sixteen ? Going at fifteen thousand."

" No, no!" cried the Princess, in terrible confusion, flying toward the nearest door opening into the rear hall-way.

" Five hundred, then," said the imperturbable outcrier, " the lady in the veil withdrawing her bid and herself too." A remark by no means intended to be disrespectful, but only by way of keeping up that constant practice of jocularity supposed to be the first requisite of a successful outcrier. Then he rang the changes and exhausted every inflection on the five hundred sestertia bid by Ignotus, and ended by knocking down to him the entire remaining contents of the palace for this sum. Adding this to his previous biddings, the total purchases amounted to about fifteen hundred sestertia, which Ignotus paid on the spot, in the currency of the realm, and the sale was declared at an end.

The Little Lady did not recover from the shock she had sustained for a considerable time. The sudden set back from the flood tide of over-values to the dead low-water mark of that contemptible five hundred sestertia had almost deprived her of her senses. When she came to herself and re-entered the apartment, she found that everything was over; the outcrier had gone, and nothing was to be seen of Vindex or his attendant.

" I suppose, Patella," said the Princess, " they will be coming for everything to-morrow."

"No, my lady, just as they were going out, the old gentleman with the bright eyes,—you mind who I mean— "

" Yes, yes, what of him ? "

" He came to me and handed me this," showing a handsome guerdon in the standard currency, "and said :—' Keep everything safe, as you would for your mistress, nothing is to go away '—and then he turned on his heel and went with the rest of them."

" What does all this mean ? " said the Princess, turning to Prima.

" I cannot imagine," said Prima, " but I am very sure Vindex knows all about it."

" Then it is infamous! How can he know all about it, unless he is a traitor to your father? Let us get home, as quickly as possible, and see what can be done this evening to prevent this fearful sacrifice."

The Prince came home with a beaming face ; he brought a large and well-filled envelope, sealed with several seals, and directed to the Princess, which he said Vindex had charged him to deliver to her.

The name of Vindex was distasteful to the Princess, in her present frame of mind ; she handed the package to Prima, who opened it and produced a bulky document, which the Princess instantly recognized as the voluminous list prepared by Prima and herself, which she had forwarded to Vindex with her own hand.

" What does he want to send that back for? It

is of no use now," said the Princess, with unwonted
bitterness in her tone. "Why add insult to injury?"

"But, Mamma, there is something else here, fastened to the list, in front of it. It is partly in writing
and partly in print."

The Prince put on his eye-glasses and looked
carefully at the paper.

"It is a bill of sale," said he. "You had better
read it."

The Princess, whose curiosity was greatly excited
by the return of her list, took the document and
began to read:—

"'Know all men by these presents that I, Ignotus,'—why that is the very man who bought everything!" exclaimed the Princess.

Her husband pricked up his ears. "How could
the Princess know that," he said to himself, "when
the sale only took place this morning?" But he
would not interrupt the reading, and the Princess
continued,—

"'For and in consideration of the sum of one
sestertium, to me in hand paid by'—bless me,
here is my own name! What a falsehood! I
never paid him anything,—'the receipt whereof is
hereby acknowledged, have bargained, sold, assigned, transferred, and set over, and by these presents do bargain, sell, assign, transfer and set over
to,'—here comes my own name again—'All the
household furniture, effects, pictures, statues, works
of art, ornaments, and property of every description,

particularly specified in the annexed list marked
A,'—that is my list, which is all correct enough,
as Prima and I know very well, but what business
has this Ignotus with it?—' To have and to hold the
same, and every part and parcel thereof'—how perfectly absurd! as if I or anybody else could hold
such a great mass of stuff?—'To her, her execu-
tors, administrators, and assigns forever'—that is
dreadfully irreverent, because nobody can have
things forever. Prima, what does all this mean? Oh,
dear! can it be because I cried out fifteen thousand,
when Ignotus said five hundred? Are we all lost?"

The Prince pricked up his ears again, but before
he could speak, Prima clapped her little hands and
exclaimed :—

"I think I see through it all. Ignotus was Vindex, and Vindex was Furax, and somehow, Vindex
has got the claim of Furax, and has arranged to
have the sale at this dull time and to manage the
biddings, just in the way they were managed, so as
to get all the furniture at a low price, and now he
has turned over every bit of it to you. Of course,
you will have to pay him the money Ignotus bid,
but it is a very small sum, compared to what the
things are worth, and Vindex will wait for it, because
he is your friend and papa's."

"But it is downright dishonesty," said the Princess.

"Why is it?" asked the Prince.

"Because the creditors will not get the full value
of the furniture," said the Princess. "It does seem

to me as if Vindex were trying to cheat them all the time, under pretence of doing something for me."

"But see," said the Prince, "it doesn't harm them in the least. The sale was a public one, and duly heralded, and if they wanted the furniture, all they had to do was to go and bid for it, and buy it if they could. Furax was so keen that he got ahead of the others, and if they had bid at the sale it would only have been for his benefit, or the benefit of the present owner of his claim, because until that was paid, nothing would go to the other creditors. As all the furniture at full value did not equal his debt, they kept away and are not hurt by the sale. Prima has guessed correctly; it was a scheme of Vindex, to save everything for you, without doing the slightest injury to anybody else, and so the furniture is yours by a perfectly valid title."

"I don't understand it," said the Princess. "There is too much circumlocution and gibberish about it to suit me."

"I understand it," said Prima, "and I believe it is all perfectly right. Furax cannot complain; he got all he was entitled to when he sold his claim to Vindex; the creditors cannot complain, because they did not choose to attend the sale, and they would have got nothing if they had attended it."

"This bill of sale, as you call it," cried the Princess, after a pause, "is not valid, after all! I know that by what Vindex told me himself. I have not paid anything, ever, to this Ignotus, and nothing is valid unless you pay, except there is natural love and affection about it, and I haven't got any of that for Ignotus, and I never could have, because he is not one of my relations."

"Vindex has taken care of that," said the Prince. "When he handed me these papers he asked me to pay him a sestertium on your account, and I paid him."

"But that is not paying it to Ignotus."

"No; but, don't you see, Ignotus has acknowledged receipt of it in the bill of sale, and that binds him."

The Princess was silenced. Vindex was a cruel and ruthless benefactor.

"Then all that diving down below stairs, and mounting to the top floor and out-bidding everybody, was a contrivance of Vindex. I didn't think at the time it was a fair sale."

"How could you think anything about it?" cried the Prince; "you were not there."

"I was there," said the Princess; and then the whole story was told, at first to the dismay of the Prince, but finally to his great entertainment, as the graphic description of the Princess and Prima brought the whole scene before him.

"There is no help for it," said he, when their tale was told. "The furniture is yours, in spite of yourself."

"I suppose I must submit," said the Princess; "what can a poor ignorant woman do against a cunning old jurisconsult? He has turned the tables upon me."

" He has turned a whole house full of furniture on you, mamma," said Prima ; " and it is all yours, and by good right, and not a piece need ever go out of your possession.   I think what Vindex has done is immensely clever and immensely kind, and I shall always love him, next to you and papa, and the children—and Juventus."

" How pleased Patella will be ! " said the Princess.

And, by this final and unselfish remark, she gave an unconscious attestation to the truth that in the wonderful intertwining of human sympathies and affairs the highest and the lowliest may meet on the common ground of the heart.

# CHAPTER XX.

## THE IMPERIAL CITY'S SHAME.

IF anything in the progress of this truthful story may have raised the presumption that it has several purposes, it is certainly free from the imputation of having any plot. It is lacking in the first essential requisite of a leading villain, unless this rôle is to be ill-naturedly attributed to Domesticus. Our good Prince, with all his misfortunes, was never involved in the meshes of a secret marriage, or any other entangling alliance, in advance of his union with the Little Lady, and there is no discarded or concealed wife, or avenging female fury, to be sprung upon the Princess, or the reader, at any critical point in these pages. The path of the Little Lady was like the shining light, and so there is not an element of that whole intricate sphere of cross-purposes and counter-crimes which makes the modern detective and the Divorce Court the novelist's best friends, from which an incident can be drawn to throw its startling hues against the sober background of the well-attested facts which are the basis of this truthful narrative.

As an offset to these confessed imperfections, it may perhaps be well pleaded that the period of time

between the birth of the Little Lady and the point
at which we have now arrived, with all its vicissitudes, has been traversed with unexampled rapidity;
that the loves of Juventus and Prima, tempting a
digression into a field as flowery and as unlimited
as their own correspondence, have been rigidly,
almost rudely, condensed into the smallest compass;
and that the martial exploits in the field, the hard
service in the camp, and the occasional suffering in
the hospital, of our young soldier, have been kept
wholly out of sight. If a great deal of time has
been covered, and many years have been unrolled in
the panorama, I have not paused to dwell upon the
details of their progress, or to divert the interest
which it is hoped may have attached to the particular fortunes we are following, and which must
tax, a little longer, the indulgence of the reader.

Juventus had found active service and speedy
promotion. He had escaped fatal disaster. He had
met with a due share of rough handling, of hair-
breadth escapes, and perilous enterprises. With the
exception of an occasional flying visit to the Imperial City, he had been, during the first two years
of his service, continuously on duty. The news of
the misfortunes of the Prince reached him in the
distant camp, far down the eastern coast of Magna
Patria, where his division of the great army of the
Sisterhood was entrenched, and from which he sent
to Prima the expression at once of his regret for
the mischance which had come to the Prince,
whose foreboding farewell he had never forgotten,

and his satisfaction at feeling that he was now, more than ever, himself charged with the duty of protecting and caring for her.

Dark days had come in the progress of the fierce struggle, in which he and so many brave spirits were bearing the brunt of the desperate onset now made with renewed fury upon the forces of the Sisterhood. The strife had long ago reached the full measure and stature of a civil war, and now the theatre of two of the main contending armies was north of the invisible line. A strong invading force, led by the foremost rebel chieftain, had crossed the border, and was offering battle on the fair fields and among the hitherto peaceful valleys of the upper side. It was at this juncture, on the eve of an impending combat which might be decisive of the fate of the Sisterhood, in the seventh month of the third year in which the cruel strife had been raging, that, of a sudden, the darkest cloud which ever burst over the Imperial City discharged its fatal bolts, and wrapped the great metropolis in its dismal folds.

The city had been more than loyal to the good cause. It had given without stint. It had stood between an empty Treasury and bankruptcy. It had stopped the mouths of traitors and traducers. It had sent its many well-equipped cohorts and legions to the front. It had done all things well and nobly. But now the long waste of the war was taxing to the utmost the resources of the whole land. The red hand of carnage clutched

whatever was needed to feed the devouring flame it
had kindled.    More money and more men was the
daily cry.    The only real money, the gold and
silver, had been drained off over sea, or had disap-
peared out of sight.    Paper promises of the Sisterhood passed from hand to hand in their place.

But, while paper money might pass for real money,
there was no such thing as filling the ranks of the
fighters with paper men.    Only real men would
answer for this greatest need, and when the belligerents would pause, after a pitched battle, reeking
with blood and ghastly with wounds, to reckon the
number of their killed, wounded, and missing, by
the score of thousands, sometimes to reach the
frightful aggregate of two score thousand on both
sides, no wonder that men were more and more
needed to fill the depleted ranks.    Voluntary en-
listment had been unexampled, but the day came
when the call for involuntary service was inevitable.
Then it was that a great outcry made by some
voices in high places, denouncing conscription, was
caught up by demagogues, and echoed in lower
places, while in the Imperial City, in the very lowest
places, it came to be the secret rallying cry of dis-
affection and traitorous plots, the potent germ of a
wild, volcanic outbreak.

" Conscript " was a hateful word, and conscription
was a hated thing.    Mixed with the hatred was the
secret working of a concealed bitterness which found
in this depth of hate a lower depth, in a hatred of
the cause the conscript would be called to serve.

At last, the day came round when the drawing of conscripts for the ranks of the army must begin in the Imperial City. A great wheel was to be set up containing the names of all citizens, between twenty and forty-five years of age, with such exceptions as public functionaries, only sons of widows dependent upon them for support, and others so situated as to make exemption a humane necessity. This wheel was to be turned in public, and the names were to be drawn by a blindfolded ministrant, and when drawn the persons they indicated were bound to two years of military service, unless they could furnish a suitable substitute in the person of an able-bodied man, or could pay a stipulated sum, far beyond the means of the ordinary workingman whose daily labor was the sole source of his support.

The excitement was intense. It was said that here was a great wrong thrust upon the people. The turn of the fateful wheel would instantly wrest many a poor and honest man from wife, and children, and home, and from the peaceful industry which supported his needy family, to hurl him to the battle field, the hospital, the grave. The rich could purchase exemption with money ; the poor were helpless as sheep sold in the shambles.

Nevertheless, few of those persons who denounced the drawing were disposed to resist it by force. There were mutterings of discontent, but no open calls for concerted opposition. At the appointed hour, a thousand citizens gathered about the door of the building in which the great wheel began to

turn in the presence of the smaller number of spectators who had been admitted to witness the drawing, and the blindfolded official went on in the discharge of his duty, undisturbed and uninterrupted,
save by the occasional jokes and jeers with which the
names, as they were drawn, were recognized and
commented on by the bystanders. The crowd
was orderly and quiet, and twelve hundred names,
in all, were drawn and announced in public hearing,
and then deposited, for safe-keeping, in an iron
chest, and the day's work was ended.

Before the next day fixed for the drawing had
dawned, a different state of things was impending.

Soon after its sunrise, a body of workmen met,
according to a preconcerted plan, and began a
round of visits to the various factories, yards and
workshops, on the eastern side of the Imperial City,
compelling the laborers to break off from their work,
and to join them in their march to the place where
the hated drawing was to be resumed and continued.
Reinforced by willing or by impressed recruits, a
vast body was soon in motion, made up of the compact nucleus of workmen and the loose material
of the streets, which always makes haste to swell the
dimensions of a mob. It halted in front of the
building, within which the wheel had already begun
to revolve, and it was soon evident that a counter
revolution had begun without.

There was a short pause, the momentary lull which
precedes the bursting of a storm, and then, with headlong fury, and wild cries, and a thick cloud of mis-

siles, the mob hurled itself against the doors, broke
into the enclosure, and routed the handful of enrolling officers, who fled in dismay with battered **heads**
and limbs, and fearful, if not fatal, bruises. The invaders vainly battered the iron chest in search of
the list of conscripts, to destroy it. Failing of this,
they tore into shreds the books and papers of the
officials, broke in pieces the implements they had
used, and scattered them among the hooting crowd
outside, **who,** all alive with a demoniac frenzy,
engendered **by the first outburst of violence,** kindled
flaming **brands and torches, and set fire to the build-**
ing, tenanted though **it was by persons wholly**
unconnected with the conscription, **and burned it**
**to** ashes, keeping off, by brute force, **the** brave
rescuers who came in the way of their appointed
duty, and at **the** risk of life, to extinguish the
flames.

The news of this lawless outbreak spread through
the city which went wild with excitement. It had
been **in peril,** years before, when the pestilence
which walked **in darkness and** wasted at noonday
threatened **a fearful destruction.** Later **on, the**
fierce flames **had swept it with a conflagration,**
known in its history, ever after, **as " the great fire,"**
but never had it seen such a day as this, the deepest
disgrace of which was the inability to cope **with,**
and stamp out, at a moment's note of alarm, this
rising insurrection. The pressing needs of the
relentless strife had drawn away the soldiery; the
civic force, well ordered, well appointed, bravely

and wisely handled, and all sufficient for the ordinary needs of daily service, was inadequate to the task of a campaign against an organized revolt which, with its swift contamination of infectious rage, was about to turn the Imperial City from a peaceful community of law-abiding citizens, into a jungle where wild beasts, in howling packs, were lurking for their prey and thirsting for blood.

The mob which had sacked, and pillaged, and fired the enrolling bureau, flushed with its first victory, and inflamed with its own fury, rushed, under the lead of its organizers, to storm a great depot of arms, in the Via Secunda, one of the leading avenues in the quarter where the first movement had been made. To plunder this place, and to put the weapons of attack into the hands of the mob, would be to improvise an invading army which could occupy that whole densely populated district of the city as a base. The building was bravely defended by a little band of keepers. A shot was fired from within, upon the lawless, attacking party, and a workman who was in its front rank fell mortally wounded. This was the signal for a general onslaught. The maddened crowd, with a battle cry of curses and armed with sledges, bludgeons, and hammers, broke down doors, windows, and barriers; pelted the garrison with paving stones; flung their blazing brands into the building; and in less than an hour it was a mass of inextinguishable flames.

And now the evil spirit of brute violence was all abroad. It stirred into swift activity the vilest

instinct, the blood-scent of which was fed by a senseless hatred of the race whose wrongs were wrapped
up in the encircling horrors of the war. This was
let loose to fasten its cruel fangs, all at once and in
this hour of darkness, upon such poor, helpless objects of its rage as were unwarned of their sudden
peril. It worked the most hideous horrors of the
dismal time. In the open streets of the Imperial
City, from lamp posts and trees, dangled the quivering bodies of these murdered victims, strangled
for their color, for whom death, without shrift, or
mercy, or a moment's warning, was dealt out by
their infuriated, persecuting foes. To the torment
of strangulation was added the torture of fire, plied
with all the savagery of the wildest tribes of red-
men. With a like frenzy, set on fire of hell, the
mob stormed, and sacked, and fired, on the first day
of the outbreak, a noble hospitium on the Via
Quinta, built to shelter and train orphan children of
the same dusky race. Seven hundred of these helpless creatures had been gathered and were cared for
within its walls, by the good genius Miserecordia
and her noble, tender band of sisters. With fiendish violence, in the broad day, the work of destruction was begun and finished by the brutal band
which, amidst the screams of the terror-stricken,
fleeing women and children, pitched its infernal
yells at a higher key, and held frantic revel in the
blazing ruin which it wrought.

A great fear fell on the Imperial City, and then a
great indignation and wrath blazed in the breast of

15

every true citizen. The city itself was powerless. Its own civil force had rallied to its rescue, with a heroism worthy of all praise. Their foremost officer had braved the dangers of the mob and been beaten off, barely escaping with his life; his chief assistant, his faithful aids, and his unflinching rank and file, had stood at every post of duty, undismayed, but powerless, in the presence of such an uprising. The great city must bear upon its brow the brand of insurrection, and be put under martial law, and trained troops be summoned, with hottest haste, to recapture it from the hands of its own lawless hordes.

The many-headed mob, having tasted the maddening draught of unrestrained license, were now not only gibbeting the dark-skinned objects of their fury, and burning and pillaging public buildings, but were bent on firing the dwellings of some obnoxious citizens, were marking others for destruction, and were turning from indiscriminate violence to organized plunder.

For three successive days the fearful struggle went on. By degrees, the military forces were concentrated against the insurgents in sufficient numbers to check them at every point, and drive them back, but only after sharp contests and hand-to-hand fighting in the streets. The rioters poured their ceaseless fire and hurled their volleys of stones from doors, windows and house-tops, finding, when repulsed, new rallying points and fresh opportunities of plunder, and inventing new methods of terror and attack, until the steady, well-drilled cohorts, with

their unflinching nerve **and** resistless will, over-
whelmed them at all points, with such slaughter
that they were scattered and put **to** flight, and **at
last,** from sheer exhaustion, relaxed their bloody and
**brutal** clutch upon the civic life.

The revolt was not, let it be **always remembered,**
at any moment, or in any sense, an uprising of **the**
people, but only a fermentation of the dregs **of the**
populace. **The** patient loyalty of the good **citi-**
zens, of every class, would have sufficed to bear **the
strain of** the conscription. It was in the cruel spite
**and hatred** toward **the** proscribed **race; the** ever-
present jealousy and grudge which the criminal and
degraded portion of the population of a great **me-**
tropolis holds in reserve against its well to do **and**
wealthier inhabitants; and in the secret sympathy for
the cause which was striving to overturn the government, that the plotters who worked in secret, and the
ruffians who filled the streets with riot, found the fuel
for the flames **they kindled.**

# CHAPTER XXI.

## DANGERS AND DELIVERANCES.

IT was on the last day of this wild carnival of insurrection that a vessel of war, bearing the starry flag of the Sisterhood, whose voyage had been northward, along the eastern shores and capes of Magna Patria, crossed the bar, sailed up the broad bay, and came to a safe mooring at a wharf at the lower end of the Imperial City, on its western side. The first person who stepped ashore was Juventus. He had been sent, at short notice, by his commanding officer, on a mission of secret military service, to the Imperial City, where he was to report according to his instructions and await orders from the seat of government. He was in the undress uniform of his command and rank, and his tall form, bronzed face, and soldierly air, made him a conspicuous figure, as he crossed the street which skirted the river, and went, with rapid steps, toward the main, broad avenue of the City.

His route lay through a narrow street, crossing a net work of crowded tenements, filled with such denizens as swarm in the degradation and filth which make the plague-spots of a metropolis. Scarcely had he set foot in this pestilent precinct before he became conscious of a sudden sound of jeers, and hootings, and derisive shouts; his way was blocked by a throng of half-clad, begrimed imps and blear-eyed hags, in rags and tatters, while on the edge of the motley mass, attracted by its wild outcries, rough men came pushing their way toward him with oaths and threats, and from the whole crowd, in one shrill, united shriek, went up a cry for his blood.

Juventus was in the hands of the mob; its spirit now diffused, as by a secret electric current, through all the vilest elements of the population, could improvise at any moment, and at any point where its material existed, a force for its foul and fiendish work. The sight of the blue uniform of a soldier of the Sisterhood was a sure and swift incentive for its cruel and bloody outburst.

In his ignorance of the cause of this strange, hostile demonstration, Juventus was dazed and stupefied. Had he landed in the great, loyal metropolis of his country, or was he, by some strange mischance, thrown into the streets of one of the capitals of the revolting sisters? He could hardly tell, but the present danger must be met, and he braced himself against the wall of the building by the side of which he was passing when so unexpectedly stopped, and tried to silence the shouts which were deafening him, by demanding in a loud voice why he was interfered with? He called upon the crowd to give way and let him pass, using, at the same time, all his strength to make a pathway for himself. A storm of jeers was all the answer he evoked; foul

words and filthy missiles flew thick and fast; while
the men who now confronted him, with savage jeers,
he saw were fully able to overpower him.   His life
was in their hands, but he would sell it dearly.

He was just gathering his strength for a desperate
struggle when his watch was demanded, and in the
same breath, his money.   From the furtive glances
and lowered tones of the foremost ruffians, he
gathered, in an instant, the idea that they intended
to possess themselves of the booty to be gained by
plundering him of his valuables, for their own benefit, before delivering him over to the mercies of the
mob.   His watch he would never give up—it was
Prima's gift—but, quick as thought, he drew, from
the inner breast pocket of his coat, a roll of bills
amounting to several hundred sestertia, and separating them, as he pulled them forth, he flung them
broadcast, into the crowd.   In an instant, and with
a wilder yell than he had yet heard, the whole devil-
ish pack turned upon itself, to catch and seize the
descending shower, and to scramble and fight for
the treasure so suddenly dispensed.   The crowd
gave way from the wall of the building against which
he stood; he slipped past, and without the slightest
sense of shame, took to his heels, with such fleetness
of foot that before the mad struggle for the money
was over, he was beyond reach, and had gained the
thoroughfare he sought.

Here he found, to his surprise, that no public
conveyances were in sight.   The usually thronged
street was almost deserted.   He hailed the only

vehicle to be seen, driven by a drayman, beside
whom he seated himself, and asked an explanation of the mystery of iniquity he had so strangely
encountered. It was quickly given, and Juventus,
as quickly, secured a promise from his companion
to take him, forthwith, to the headquarters of the
military forces to which the City, being under martial law, was now subject.

" I must have a hand in this fight," said Juventus,
with a voice and air of prowess which made the
drayman think he carried Cæsar.

The appearance of an officer, fresh from the battle-
fields where the strife for the Sisterhood was raging,
with his ready offer of instant service, was most
opportune, for the need of skilled commanders was
very great. Juventus lost no time in assuming the
duties assigned him, and within two hours from the
time of his deliverance from the mob, he was at the
head of a corps of sharp-shooters, opening upon a
horde of the rioters a destructive fire, before which
they fled in terror and despair.

The conflict was almost ended ; but after night-fall,
tidings came that the insurgents had rallied, in
great numbers, as if for a final onslaught, and were
pillaging and plundering, in a quarter of the City
where the force of soldiery detailed to disperse them
had proved too weak, and had been repulsed with
serious loss, leaving some of their number dead in
the streets. The crisis was imminent. This new
stronghold of the rioters was on two of the avenues,
on the eastern side, running parallel to each other,

and in the streets crossing them at right angles; both avenues and streets being designated by numbers, according to the method of the Imperial City in its northernmost districts, the avenues held by the rioters being the Via Prima and the Via Secunda, and the streets, those ranging from twenty-third to twenty-ninth, in numerical order.

Juventus and his command were ordered to the scene of this fresh victory of the mob and reaching it by a quick march, found the hostile forces in full possession of many of the houses along the Via Secunda, and in the adjacent streets, posted at the windows, and on the roofs, whence their aim could be sure and deadly, and their destructive missiles hurled with murderous effect.

Juventus gave orders to his men, first to sweep the streets with their fire, and then to turn it upon the windows and house-tops, moving forward steadily along the line held by the mob. A terrible battle ensued. The streets were cleared and the rioters turned into a howling, fleeing mass, in which the dead and the wounded were trampled upon by the terror-stricken fugitives; while the shots fired from the close ranks of the soldiery, at the houses, windows, and roofs, took fatal effect.

The insurgents, driven from the houses, took to the streets, and the fighting went on, at close quarters, ending with the flight of the now thoroughly panic-stricken and beaten mob. Juventus ordered a close pursuit in the main avenue, and a clearing of the side streets, to prevent the rallying of the broken forces of the enemy. He turned a detachment of his men into one of the streets, at the corner of which, from a tall house, some of the sharpest firing had come. As he halted to let his men go by, and to see that nothing endangered the rear of the column, a blow from behind, whether dealt close at hand, or by a stone hurled from above, he never knew, struck him to the ground. He sprang to his feet, with a dizzy and confused brain ; in the darkness of the night, left for the moment without the power of speech,—hardly with the power of thought, —he could give no word of command, or call for aid ; his men, unwitting of his disaster, pushed on in their pursuit while he felt himself caught by strong hands, and knew, upon regaining full consciousness, that he was helpless, and a prisoner.

Although powerless to resist, the first feeling of Juventus, on coming to a clear comprehension of his position, was that of surprise that he had not been killed outright, but as the experience of the morning had taught him that the greed of gain was, with many of the brutal band of rioters, a stronger motive than the thirst for revenge, he thought it possible he was to be held for ransom. Not a word was spoken as he was led by his captors through a door-way level with the street, into the long narrow hall of the high building, already mentioned, from the upper windows of which he had marked that a murderous and persistent fire had been kept up, until silenced by the fatal, answering shots from his own ranks.

There was a dim light in the passage, and as he was hurried past the narrow stair-way, he caught sight of the flashing eyes of a woman who stood on the landing above, looking down upon him, her face enveloped in a black wrap, and her form quivering from head to foot. Beyond the stair-way, and underneath it, were steps leading to the cellar of the house, and after descending these he was conducted to the rear vault, into which he was thrust, and left in utter darkness.

His brain was not yet entirely clear, and sharp pains shot through it. He threw off his cap, and pressed his hands against his head, to make sure there was no fracture or contusion, and then he groped about his prison, to discover its limits and possible openings. It was simply a vault for coal, a heap of which he soon encountered. It had, in the rear, an open shaft, bricked on all sides and covered at the top with an iron grating. The sole egress from the vault was the door by which he had entered, now locked on the outside.

How long a time passed after he finished this exploration and while he sat in the darkness, or what were the thoughts which filled and crowded his mind, in its bewilderment and uncertainty, he could never tell. In the retrospect it seemed a dismal blank, but he never forgot his sudden recall to the keenest exercise of his senses when he caught the sound of footsteps, and of what seemed a slow tramp overhead, and presently, of digging in the earth, just beyond the open grating. It crossed his mind that perhaps his own grave was in preparation, and he felt, more than ever, how futile resistance would be. Quickened by this new sense of danger, he listened more eagerly, and perceived that the work of digging went on in dead silence, not a word being uttered, nor a sound made, save by the dull, monotonous spade-thrusts. Just at this moment, he was conscious of a faint, rustling noise, and the turning of a key; then he heard his own name breathed in a whisper so soft as to convey a command of silence as well as a summons.

In the darkness, he could not discern the speaker, but he sprang forward toward the door; the instinct of self-preservation restraining him from any spoken word. Extending his hand, he felt it grasped by another hand, quivering and icy cold. Yielding to its guidance, he was led to the front of the underground passage, and there his unseen deliverer spoke.

"Juventus, I am Stella. I saw you when they brought you in. I have been planning—ever since—to save you. I think they mean to kill you. One of them wants money so much, he may keep them from it. But do as I say. Here are overalls, a workman's blouse, and an old hat. Put them on over your uniform. Here is a spade. Take it and follow me. They are digging graves, behind the house, for two who were shot. They are afraid the place will be searched in the morning, and they must bury them now. They needed another man to help in the digging, and I said I would fetch him from close

by. You must dig; they will not dare say a word.
They will want you to go when the digging is done,
because they will let no one into the secret of their
having imprisoned you here. I will pay you when
you quit the work, and you will walk out free."

"But, Stella," said Juventus, who was already
equipped in his disguise, "why cannot I walk out
now?"

"Go," said she, in a quivering whisper, "but then
they will kill me for your escape."

"Pardon me, my brave Stella," said Juventus, "I
am only half myself. I will do what you say. Nay,
I will not—I will go back to the vault—unless I
know that you will be safe. May they not, in any
case, suspect you of aiding my flight?"

"No, no," said Stella. "I had a key to the door,
they did not know of. I have left it inside, on
the floor. They will think you found it; I have un-
fastened the grating, here in front, from below.
That will account for your getting out."

"But they will want you to show the man whom
you got to help in the digging."

"I have a good friend who will swear he did it, if
need be. No, they will never suspect me. Juventus,"
and her whisper was still more quivering, "one of
the men who was shot was my husband; he is dead;
—he was good to me—when he was himself—I was
as fierce for revenge as any of them—they think I
am now—but why should you be killed or harmed?
you saved my life—I am only paying a debt; but
quick—come now."

Taking him again by the hand and ascending
the stairs, she led him, in the dark, to the rear door;
a single descending step brought them into the little
space of ground behind the house, enclosed by high
board fences, where two men were digging, side by
side. The coming of Juventus with his spade was
evidently expected, and his falling into the hard
work, with vigor, was accepted in silence.

The night was dark and rain was falling, so that
he could not see the faces of his co-workers, but he
dug with all his might, thankful that in case of any
miscarriage of Stella's plan, he had a new weapon in
his hand,—his sword and pistols having been taken
from him at his capture. At the moment, he was
more anxious for Stella than for himself, knowing
that her safety depended on the successful issue of
her stratagem. Accordingly, he put into his task
all of the dogged persistence of the class of which
he was, for the time being, an ally, and the two
graves were soon dug to their proper depth. He
paused, resting on his spade, and awaited the next
movement with an intense apprehension which could
not have been concealed but for the darkness of the
night.

To his inexpressible relief, after a whispered word
from one of his fellow-diggers to Stella, who meanwhile handed to the speaker a heavy key, she thrust
into his hand a bit of paper, representing a fraction
of a sestertium, and the ruffian with the key
motioned Juventus to follow. He led the way, in
silence, through the long hall, until they reached

the street door, which he unlocked and opened, just
wide enough to permit the egress of Juventus, who
walked forth into the dark and silent street, a free
man.

Keeping fast hold of his trusty spade, he went,
with rapid strides, toward the main thoroughfares,
exciting no observation, and encountering few persons, as the night was well advanced, and the citizens
did not care to be abroad in these troublous times.

He was seized with an irresistible longing to see
Prima.   On the morrow he must resume the duty
of his mission, so strangely interrupted, and, perhaps, be ordered to a distance.   The events which
had crowded themselves into this single day, between sunrise and midnight, were so strange ; his
double deliverance from a cruel death, or from a
great danger, seemed so signal a blessing ; the good
part he had been able to take in the suppression of
the insurrection was such a wonderful opportunity
of service, that he was hardly able to believe these
things were all embraced within the compass of a
few hours.   He must tell the story, at once, to her
for whom his life had been so signally spared, and
in the intense excitement of his feelings, was carried so far beyond his real strength that it seemed
to him an easy thing to overcome the distance
which separated him from the dwelling of the
Prince.

In fact, it was a long and weary way to traverse,
at so late an hour, for one in the physical condition
in which the day's vicissitudes had left Juventus

But finding that in the upper part of the city, on its western side, removed from the scene of the riots, the public vehicles were running, and that the last northward trip for the night was about to be made, he was enabled, by the use of the bit of currency which Stella had placed in his hand, to be conveyed to a point near the round tower described to him by Prima, and thence he came, without difficulty, to the willow trees and the gate they overshadowed.

The house faced toward the West and North ; as Juventus entered the gate, he saw that a light was burning in a window of its front, left open for the chance breezes of the summer night. As he paused on the gravel-path, the wind, which had risen in the night and changed from its rainy quarter, blew off the lingering clouds, and far up, in the dim heavens, he caught the distant flicker of the North Star. At this moment, at the open casement, he saw with throbbing heart, a white-robed figure, and there fell upon his ear the words, breathed toward the far-off orb,—

"Good-night, Juventus."

"Good-night, Prima," was his quick response.

He saw her start ; he heard her sudden cry of wonder ; and fearing she might be overcome by the startling sound, called with louder voice, to declare his presence, and to reassure her perturbed spirit.

Then he said, "If it is too late, do not let any one be disturbed ; I could not go without greeting you, even if the greeting be a farewell."

"No one will be disturbed," said Prima, "and no

one would forgive you had you not come. Mamma is still astir. In these fearful times we have not been able to sleep; we will all come down and meet you at the door; wait only a few moments."

The long day's work was done. Its terrible successive strains had been met, and they were overpast. The quiet home of his betrothed had been gained in safety; her dear voice had welcomed him; no further need of strength, of will, of courage, of excitement, to bear him up for any deed of daring or duty. The reaction came with sudden force, and as the Prince and the Princess with Prima, all aroused and eager to receive the unexpected visitor, threw open their door for his entrance, he could only take one tottering step forward, and then fell senseless at their feet.

# CHAPTER XXII.

## THE VIA SEXTA.

A T last, after four years of fighting, the strife was ended. The last shot had been fired; the final surrender made; and the Sisterhood was saved. Following swiftly upon the suppression of the riots in the Imperial City, came the issue of the impending battle upon which, more than upon any previous conflict, hung the issues of the war. It had resulted, not in the destruction of the invading army, or its capture, but in checking its advance and forcing its withdrawal to the nether side of the line, there to re-intrench itself for new resistance; while, over the wide theatre of the strife, renewed hostilities and campaigns on a more extended scale gave still vaster proportions than ever before to the gigantic struggle.

Months earlier, with much hesitation and after many sad reverses, the real issue had been reached and the blow struck whereby the knot, which statesmanship could not untie, and which contention had only tightened, was severed by the sword. As a final measure of war, and after a hundred days of warning, the word had gone forth which, with the dawn of the new year, proclaimed the enfranchisement of a race.

16                                          241

At last, the leaders, long waited for and trained by the lessons of the defeats which those who went before them had suffered, as well as by the victories they themselves had won, came to the front, to finish the bloody work. Then, under the supreme command of one patient, unflinching, steady will, the dread issue was forced to its final trial, and the day dawned when the old flag floated once more over all the rescued realm.

The youth and vigor of Juventus had saved him from more than a temporary shock to his nervous system, as the result of his day spent among the infuriated rioters of the Imperial City. The care of the Princess and Prima restored him to health even more quickly than suited them, for his impatience to resume his distant command outstripped their loving anxieties for his complete recovery, and took him from them, before they were quite ready to trust him to himself. His services on the eventful day were duly recognized and honorably mentioned, and by the timely intervention of the Prince, prompted by the papers he found in the possession of Juventus, the special service on which he came to the Imperial City suffered no harm. The secret of his strange deliverance he confided only to Prima, fearing that if entrusted to other ears some possible danger might come to his deliverer. All that was generally known was that he had been left wounded in the street, and had, afterwards, made his way to the house of the Prince.

The war ended, the great contending armies were disbanded. In the strange and almost instantaneous transformation from serried hostile ranks to peaceful tillers of the soil, or toilers in all the countless arts, and industries, and professions in which, the broad land over, the labor of her sons was engaged, the world saw a new sight. Peace, as with an enchanter's touch, dissolved the whole hideous array and enginery of war.

So have we seen, from some high peak, the black, storm-charged billows of cloud, heaving and surging with seemingly inexhaustible stores of pent-up wrath, on a sudden melt away at the sovereign glance and beam of the outbursting sun.

Juventus was glad to return unharmed and with a brilliant record to his accustomed work as a civilian. He found, without difficulty, a new opening in the activities which immediately received a fresh impulse at the restoration of peace, and was soon regularly employed, as the head of a department, in an important industrial enterprise.

He pleaded with Prima for a speedy marriage. He thought he had reason on his side when he urged that hostilities being ended, engagements should cease, and union should be the paramount idea. He had saved, out of his pay, enough to provide for the fitting-up of the modest establishment which he proposed. He unfolded his plans to Prima with the courage of a veteran campaigner. To condense in a few words the conversations and discussions of several evenings,—he had projected an alli-

ance with a comrade who had served with him in
the war, and who owned a house in the Via Sexta,
a thoroughfare which, though next in order and
parallel to the Via Quinta, was separated from it by
an impassable gulf, in respect of gentility and of
permitted residence, under the rules of Societas.

It was not, however, at that time, as to any part
of it, under a special ban of disrepute, and was
largely devoted to the uses of small traders, and as
yet unvisited by the marvelous methods of upper-
level locomotion, to which, later on, it was appro-
priated.  The house was occupied on the ground
floor by the comrade, the front portion being available for his business as an engraver and carver in
metals, and the rear for the living apartments of
himself and wife.  Overhead, was a suite of rooms
of which Juventus would become the tenant, and
which could be fitted-up to suit the needs of Prima
and himself.

Prima had not faced the cannon's mouth on the
battle-field, but she had the quiet courage needful
to brave the galling fusilade to which she knew she
would be subjected if she took up the line of march
to which Juventus invited.  To marry a poor man
whose fortune was all to be made, and whose daily
earnings must suffice for their whole support, to live
outside of the limits of Societas, to exchange, for
the friendly greetings of its votaries, their sneers
and shrugs, and ill-concealed—perhaps openly
expressed—disdain, none but a brave girl would
dare.  And such an one was Prima.  Juventus dis-

closed his whole scheme. He figured out, to a
sestertium, the yearly, monthly, daily cost of the
living, and brought his practical mathematics to
bear on the problem of making both ends so meet
that there would be considerable lapping over.

"I have enough on hand," said he, "to make
those bare rooms, with the added touch of your
taste and skill, as attractive as if they were in a
wing of the bravest palace on earth ; as good books
can be put on pine shelves daintily draped, as in
the grandest library ; as good cheer can be found
in the cosy corner where our board is to be spread,
as in the most luxurious banqueting-hall ; there can
be place always for two, beside ourselves, whether
our table be square or round, and if we cannot
pour libations of sparkling Falernian into gemmed
goblets, we can provide from some honest, though
rougher vintage for the guests we entertain. A man
surely has a right to take some risks in the
line which I have marked out. So long as I can
earn enough, and more than enough, for our support, in this frugal way, why should we not begin at
once the journey of our married life ?"

"Mamma thinks," said Prima, "and often says, that
girls who have been brought up in luxury lose a
great deal by never having the opportunity of
beginning at the beginning, as so many of the very
best people did who have liberal homes in their later
days, to which they grew up gradually. For children
to commence where their parents leave off, seems
to her to be burning the candle at the wrong end.

There is nothing more to be had if you have every-thing at once. And then it seems to happen, so often, that they who commence at the very top have to come down to the very bottom, or unpleasantly near it, without the preparation of a previous experience. There must be a great deal of pleasure in making one's way from small beginnings. For my own part I don't want to start as a dowager."

" I have no fear," said Juventus, "that we shall not move as rapidly as may be desirable toward greater comfort than we may find at first ; but to keep within the bounds which are indispensable now, will require some sacrifice, and if what I am propos-ing is to be a trial, I will not ask you to assent. I will wait as long as you require ; not as patiently, perhaps, as you could wish."

" Possibly," said Prima, " we could do a little missionary work, by way of setting an example to some of these other young people, who run to the very edge of the sea of matrimony, and then rush back, because they are afraid to venture into the waves without having the life-preserver of a fortune tied about them. Of course," she said, demurely, " I must see this thing in the light of a positive duty."

" You will do what I ask ? I am sure you will ! " said Juventus, with a whole sunrise of hope in his eyes.

" I will," said Prima ; and it was a bargain, not signed, to be sure, but sealed in a sufficiently bind-ing way, according to the immemorial usage of

Magna Patria and other realms, and to the satisfaction of both the contracting parties.

"And what now, Prima?" asked Gloriosa, when they met, for the first time, after the event I have just recorded.

"Juventus and I are to be married next month," said Prima. "He has found excellent employment, and has taken some very nice rooms in the Via Sexta."

"The Via Sexta!" cried Gloriosa, throwing up both hands, heavy with their sparkling, gold-encased diamonds and rubies, in a way that expressed unutterable horror.

"Yes," said Prima; "you could hardly expect him to take a palace on the Via Quinta, considering that he only earns, just now, less than two hundred sestertia a month."

"And you are going to be married on that?"

"Why not? It is enough to begin on. The rooms are lovely. They are over the shop of an engraver who served in the war with Juventus. His wife is a most capable little woman, and she will supply all we want, and keep our one servant, besides."

"This is horrible, absolutely horrible!" said Gloriosa. "You are going to destroy yourself. Why not wait till he can support you decently?"

"He can support me decently now," said Prima. "He is in love with me and I am in love with him. He earns enough to keep us both, in a simple way. I can help him in his work. I am ready to share his

fortunes, and I cannot see why we should wait on
the whims of other people when doing as we prefer
helps us, and does not harm them."

" It is madness," said Gloriosa. " Think of what
you have been accustomed to, and what you are enjoying, even now, luxury,—or comfort, at least,—
and the height of respectability, although, just at this
moment, you are off the Avenue. And now you
want to sacrifice yourself for a man who has nothing.

" He has everything," said Prima, " except money,
and that will come, in good time. I am making no
sacrifice in casting in my lot with him. I am not
losing, but gaining. What did I read, only the
other day, in the rude French of an old chanson,
earlier than Charlemagne—a single line which tells
the whole truth, for all time—

" *'Li cuers d'un hom vaut tout l'or d'un pais.'*
' The heart of a man is worth all the gold of a land.'
We do not live up to this barbaric standard. With
us, the love of gold eats at the very core. The
heart of a man is thrown into the scale, against
money, to be outweighed and held for naught.
Come what may, I will stand by my choice of a
man's heart."

"A man's heart, without a man's purse, will furnish nothing but sentiment which pays no bills,"
said Gloriosa.

" I know that well enough," said Prima, " and I
have seen girls rush foolishly into marriage, to find
out their mistake too late, if not too soon. But,
Gloriosa, is it not true that, almost always, the risk

they took was of the man and not of his means?
That is my risk and I have measured it. If Juventus were as rich as the richest, I would still want to
marry not his money but himself; and how if a man
loses his money, as so many do and must ? Suppose Novus were to lose his fortune—"

"I am independent," said Gloriosa, quickly and
somewhat sharply. "There was a settlement before
we were married. That was a condition."

Prima was sorry she had made this personal allu-
sion for she should have remembered that the ties
of domesticity were said to sit very lightly on
Novus, and it was matter of general knowledge that
Gloriosa's recognized independence was asserted in a
variety of ways.

"Forgive me," she said, "I had no right to ask
questions. All I meant was that where a man
has nothing to give but his heart, and his best endeavors, a girl may take the risk of marriage, if he
is able to earn daily bread for himself and any one
dependent upon him. This is a risk people are
taking every day, in humbler spheres than yours
and mine, and are we to be shut out from a kind of
happiness they are permitted to enjoy?"

"Yes," said Gloriosa, "of course we are, unless we
are willing to go down to their level. We are just
as much shut out from what you call their happiness as they are from what, I suppose, they call our
extravagance. Of course, you can degrade yourself, if you choose, but you must take the consequences."

" There is no degradation," retorted Prima; " I can
live as pure and noble a life in a humble place, and
among poor people, as I could in the Via Quinta,
and I am glad of the opportunity of doing it.
What right have you now, or had I once, to anything
more than the poorest?   Good fortune and great
fortunes seem to me, more and more, purely acci-
dental, except when they come from one's own
creative efforts.   I would rather have a single sestertium in my hand that I had earned, or that some
one I loved had earned for love of me, than a hundred that I might get by gift or inheritance."

" What nonsense, Prima!  Do you mean you would
rather enlist under Domesticus, and go out to service, than live at home as you do, or as you have
done ? "

" No.  Although I would even do that, if I could
do nothing else and had to gain my own living,
before I would lie down and die of inaction.   There
is not the wide difference in service, or work, which
you imagine.   What is the real difference between
putting food into a child's mouth to nourish his
body, as any nurse may do when she puts a bib
under his chin and a spoon in his fingers, and putting high thoughts into his mind, as the great pre-
late did when he chronicled the wanderings of
Ulysses for the heir of the Gallic throne, and placed
an immortal classic in his hand ? "

" All the difference," said Gloriosa, " that there is
between the lowest and the highest of any kind of
effort."

" Precisely," said Prima ; " but the same in kind, essentially; and the great advantage we enjoy is that our service, if we are called to render it, may be of the finer grade and grain. I can make beds, and make bread, thanks to old Patella who has taught me, but I can do other things which rank higher than these humble ministries, and are more elevating, and command better rewards. In their place, the lowliest labor and the lowest laborer stand on their own merits, and if their work is good and true they should be respected accordingly. I really believe one reason why this never-ending question of Domesticus is so troublesome, is because so many people have never stopped to think of anything except the obligations of those who serve, taking no account of the reciprocal obligation of those who are served. The best-bred men and women are the first to acknowledge this, and I know very well that, shiftless and short-sighted and slow-handed as the emissaries of Domesticus may be, they are quick to discern the difference between true gentility and its counterfeit, between a real lady and a make-believe one."

" For all that, Prima, I think you are very ungrateful to talk as you do. I cannot fancy, marriage aside, you would really prefer a life of labor to living at home."

" I do not say I would. It is lovely to feel you are free in your father's house, but this world is full of changes, and it is well, I think, for every one to have in themselves, and to be sure they have, the will and capacity to make their own way, in spite of circumstance and adverse fate. I tell you, Gloriosa, the very first time I ever tried to support myself, just a tiny little bit, I felt a kind of satisfaction in being able to do it that was like a new sense of life."

" What in the world did you do ? "

" I just wrote out, almost in his own words, a wild sea story that one of the old fishermen told me, when we were down at the coast, and I worked in a description of his cabin, with every queer thing that was in it and about it, and had the good luck to have it accepted where such things are turned into money. Of course, it was not much, but it was mine."

" Well, Prima, plain as your path may seem to you, I cannot follow you in it. If you are going to ostracize yourself, and go outside the pale of Societas, go you must, but nobody will call on you in the Via Sexta."

" We shall see," said Prima. " I shall not expect any pretty little men, nor any imitation ladies, but Juventus has friends who will not desert him, and I thought I had some who would not desert me."

" You are so unreasonable," said Gloriosa. " Imagine my chariot at a shop-door for an afternoon call !"

" I shall not tax my imagination at the expense of your friendship," said Prima.

" It is not a question of friendship," said Gloriosa, rising to depart. " It is a question of social order.

You want to set Societas at defiance, and nobody is strong enough for that. Anything, or anywhere, in a side street will do, but over a shop is almost as bad as in the slums."

"I am not going to be angry with you," said Prima, "no matter how ill you treat me, but you know very well the Via Sexta is not in the slums. Nor do I want to set Societas at defiance. How absurd for me, or for any one else, to run a tilt against that great goddess whom all the gay world worships. Only I will not be pressed into her hard service. No one can love better than I do the friendliness of true social intercourse. It is the very life of life. There are plenty of men and women in the train of Societas who are as good as gold, and as true as steel—dear friends of yours and mine—whose praise is always on our lips. I have no quarrel with them, but solely with the system of which they make themselves a part, and which they uphold in what seems to me its vicious methods. There is as much difference between genuine social friendship and its counterfeit in the circles of Societas, as there is between the white and red of Nature on the cheek of a young girl in the morning sunshine, and the chalk and rouge of the tiring-room, made ghastly by the glare of the footlights."

Gloriosa shrugged her ample shoulders. "If you are going into a tirade against cosmetics, I don't know where you will stop. The next thing you will disavow your belief in the three Graces. But, Prima, I must be going. I am making visits, and could not have stopped so long with you but that I ran short of Novus' tablets. At my last call I had to leave five of his; to be sure, it was an extra-sized family, married daughters living at home, and all that."

"Considering that Novus never actually calls anywhere, under any circumstances," said Prima, "leaving five of his tablets seems like a great deal of fiction founded on no fact. But since when has there been such an increase in the number of tablets distributable at front doors?"

"The edict is only a little more rigidly enforced this season," said Gloriosa. "It has been duly promulgated by that high-priestess of Societas, Bona Forma, who is charged with the regulation of these matters. Societas will not be tied to a constitution or a code, but she makes and unmakes general rules, and this is rule number twelve million and twenty-six. I know it by heart. It requires that in the interchange of tablets one must be left by, and for, and upon, every person of proper age, enrolled and capable of duty in the ranks of Societas, provided that the tablets of gentlewomen shall be left only for, and upon, persons of the above description of their own sex, and the tablets of men for, and upon, persons of the like description of both sexes, unmarried men excepted. Of course, everybody whose tablet is left is not supposed to have called in person. It is simply saying you called when you didn't call; but that is all right by every rule of Societas, written or unwritten. And now, Prima, I

have given you fair warning, and I mean what I
have said. You are going to put yourself out of
the pale, and as long as you persist in your insane
ways we must treat you accordingly. I don't
believe you will be as bad as you threaten, so I
wish you good-bye, and a better mind."

" Good-bye," said Prima, and they parted with a
kiss, in which the fervor of their old friendship
seemed, to each of them, to have been checked
by a sudden chill.

# CHAPTER XXIII.

## A MARRIAGE NOT À LA MODE.

JUVENTUS and Prima were married in the early days of Autumn, in a quiet way, quite at variance with the prevailing fashion of the Imperial City in the matter of weddings. There were a few friends, a few flowers, and a few presents. Gloriosa sent her greetings, in spite of her disapproval, from the sea-side metropolis where she was revolving in a whirligig of festivities, almost as exciting and as exacting as those of the Imperial City at the height of its gayest season, and with them, a colossal souvenir which Prima thought would seem strangely out of keeping with the modest conditions of Via Sexta.

"How very apt people are to resemble their presents!" said the Princess to Prima, when this elaborate piece was unpacked. "Gloriosa is nothing if not beyond bounds, and this efflorescent epergne, with its outspreading branches, calls for a table at least six feet wide and pulled out for fourteen people."

"It is lovely in her to have sent it," said Prima, "and certainly it is very handsome. I shall hope to be able to live up to it some day. But I am so glad that, as we are placed just now, we are rid of the conventional present, and that Societas has levied no assessment for my benefit on any of her members. How charming are these little remembrances which express real affection! I had no idea so many of my old friends would keep me in mind; and nothing touches me more than this wonderful catch-bag which old Patella has worked, with its marvels of embroidery."

"I wonder where Stella is," said the Princess. "I would be so glad to have her here."

Patella had tried, at the instance of Prima, to discover the whereabouts of Stella, but thus far in vain. She had left the house, and apparently the neighborhood, in which she had lived after her marriage, and no one could be found who knew whither she had gone.

The wedding over, and the short trip which followed it ended, the newly-married pair took possession of their home in the Via Sexta, not without many strivings of heart on the part of the Prince and the Little Lady, to whom, in the changed condition of their affairs, the marriage of Prima and her departure from their loving care and companionship, almost empty-handed, and to so lowly a home, was the sorest trial they had encountered.

The Prince had, at first, been unwilling to accede to the plans of Juventus. He foresaw many objections and difficulties, even after the Princess had been won over to the side of the adventurous lovers.

17

He pleaded for a side street, and thought the combined effect of the Via Sexta and the shop would be fatal to the social prospects of the young couple.

"I thought so, myself," said the Princess, "but Juventus declares he has walked a hundred miles in the side streets, and explored innumerable houses; the result is he must spend the bulk of his pay for rent, or go where that single item will not eat up all his earnings. He wants to be within walking distance of his work, and his whole future hinges on the question of rent. We are all the time crying out against the obstacles the high prices put in the way of the marrying of young people. Here you have a couple with courage enough to accept the only possible solution."

"If the house must be in the Via Sexta, I wish it might be on a corner, with the entrance on the side street," said the Prince; "that would be a kind of compromise."

"You will never get Juventus, nor Prima, to make compromises for the sake of their footing with Societas. They will hold their ground and their one flight up, against a world in arms. A girl may go from the Via Quinta, three thousand miles, to a cattle ranch in Ultima Occidente, and her bravery will be applauded. Is the quiet, stay-at-home courage which takes Prima a single block off, to be followed with hisses and cat-calls?"

"It surely will be," replied the Prince, "because Societas draws her strictest lines at just such points

as this, and forbids the bans where a couple propose to live without her limits, in order to live
within their means."

"In other words," cried the Princess, "Societas
will permit every sacrifice at her own shrine, but
none at the old altar fires of the heart!"

"Of course," said the Prince, "there is no more
sentiment about Societas than there is about a dia-
mond-broker, but no end of shrewdness and practical wisdom. Aside from all that, these children
are taking a considerable risk. Juventus may be
stricken down with illness—many a man is."

"He is not very likely to be," said the Princess.
"He went through the war without any serious
injury; he is in good health, and will be much
more likely to keep so if he has a comfortable
home and regular hours, a bright fireside and a
loving wife."

"He may be killed, or meet with some accident."

"Then Prima can come to us; besides, there are
the great guilds which provide for such emergen-
cies, and Juventus has already made arrangements
with them."

The Prince suggested that in the account current
of married people the most formidable debit item
might be a baby.

The Little Lady had never been frightened by a
baby, and never meant to be. Twins had no terrors
for her.

The Prince was silenced, though not convinced;
and he gave Prima away, with some misgivings,

and yet satisfied, in his heart of hearts, that the pledges Juventus had given to fortune when his marriage vows were uttered would surely be redeemed.

Brighter days were at hand for the Prince.

The new era of peace and prosperity which followed the ending of the strife brought with it a great increase in the values of property, and opened a wide door for every description of renewed activity.

The great tidal wave of inflation, following on the permanent exchange of paper promises for gold coin, lifted things which had been supposed to be mere wreckage and drift-wood into values which were as unexpected as they were excessive. In the Imperial City, vast public improvements were projected and carried forward, especially in the quarter which included the lands of the Prince; and as the sequel of what seemed, at the outset, the unreasoning obstinacy of the Little Lady, resulting in the withholding of these lands from sale, the time came when their new value made it easy to provide for the bulk of his whole outstanding indebtedness, after applying his other means of payment to the satisfaction of his creditors.

Some fortunate events, among which was the reclamation of a large quantity of the staple product of the nether side of the invisible line, shipped to him by his chief debtors, just at the breaking out of the strife, and so intercepted that it had been held, during all the

years of the conflict, without capture or destruction,
aided to swell his assets. By the good management of Vindex, the happy day came at last after
long and weary waiting, when the whole heavy load
could be lifted. The outcome was far better than
even he had ever dared to hope. The Prince would
be stripped, to be sure, of his wealth, but he would be
out of debt, and the palace was saved, so that he
could secure it to the Princess, free and clear, and
his new business alliances were such as to ensure
ample means for his comfortable living, and the possible nucleus of a fresh fortune.

The debts all satisfied, including the timely ad-
vances made by Vindex, at the time of the failure,
for the purchase of the claim of Furax, the old jurisconsult was able to assure the Little Lady that she
was the owner, in her own right, of the home she
had loved so much; that the balance due every
creditor was satisfied out of the proceeds of the other
lands, and that there was enough left to represent
her dower right, which the Prince, and not the creditors, could now make good to her by a conveyance
of the palace on the Via Quinta.

All this she understood when she united with
Assignatus, as occasion required, in signing the
deeds of the lands, as they were now sold, from time
to time. But the matter of the furniture she could
not fully comprehend. And before she would consent to re-enter the palace as its owner, she must see
Vindex face to face once more, and learn the whole
truth. The furniture, although hers from the day

and date of the bill of sale, she had never touched.
The palace had been advantageously rented and
well tenanted during most of the time since the outcry took place, and a due proportion of the rent had
been religiously reserved, by the vigilance of Vindex, for the Princess, as representing the use of her
furniture by the tenant, but even this she would
not accept.   Now that the whole tangle was about
to be unravelled, she must be sure there was no
dishonest nor doubtful thread in the confused mass.

Vindex had met the Little Lady frequently during the long interval between his first repulse in the
matter of the dower right, and the present better time,
but he had made no progress in gaining her over to
his views.   On the contrary, she had nipped in the
bud a project he had hoped to mature for a compromise with the Prince's creditors by paying sixty *per
cent.* of his debts.   After satisfying himself that it
would be accepted by the great body of the creditors,
he had broached the subject cautiously to the Princess, whose consent was necessary, as the execution
of the scheme involved the sale of the lands, free of
her dower, which he meant to provide for as a part
of the settlement.   When he had unfolded his plan,
the Princess asked, first of all :—

" Would such a settlement be honest ? "

" Most assuredly," said Vindex ; " men who fail
for over a million are not expected to pay in full."

' Then the Prince would never be out of debt ? "

" Yes ; he would be entirely out of debt ; he
would have satisfied all claims and be free to take a

fresh start. It is in the interest of the whole community that this should be the method of giving honest debtors new opportunities."

"Suppose, by new opportunity, the honest debtor retrieves his losses and becomes able to pay the deficiency; is he not bound to do it?"

"No," said Vindex, "he is not bound."

"Legally, not, I suppose," said the Princess, "but in honor and good conscience?"

"No, again. Because there is no standard by which to determine a fancied obligation resting on honor or conscience, and not on right as fixed by law. A debtor whose debt is once discharged never owes that debt again, or any part of it. If, afterward, he is so placed that, without injustice to others, he can gratify his particular sense of obligation by giving his former creditors the balance of their discharged claims, this is his own affair. He cannot gauge his action by anything save his individual choice. The community does not require or expect it of him, and he comes under no discredit or criticism for not doing it, because, in the long run, and under ordinary conditions, it is impossible, in a single life, with all its many responsibilities and vicissitudes, for a man to re-open what is closed, and to add to the necessity of meeting present demands the luxury of providing for those which have been cancelled in the past. If the law of the land discharges a man from his debts, and a supposed social law holds him undischarged, the honest debtor who has paid all he could, and whose

after-acquired means are needed for his family and
his new engagements, will never be freed, either in
the eye of his own conscience, or in the regard of
his fellows."

" I see," said the Princess; " it is purely a question
of choice, depending on the circumstances of the
individual."

" Just so," said Vindex.

" But for all that, better pay the whole than a part,
if possible."

" Of course, if the means exist."

" I believe they will exist for us," said the Princess. "And I would rather wait and take all the
chances than compromise with the creditors now
and leave any question for the future, after the fresh
start has been taken. Depend upon it, the money
will come, and then we shall pay all and be wiser
for the future. What does Novus call it when he
says that something that is going to happen happens
a month or so before it happens ? "

" I suppose he says, in the dialect of his venture-
some calling, that it has been ' discounted.' "

" Yes, that is it. Well, I think the best way to dis-
count one's debts is to pay them in full as soon as
one has the money in hand, and not leave anything
for conscience, or honor, or yourself, or other people,
to worry about in the future."

The Little Lady's prediction had now come true,
and at last Vindex felt sure that there could be no
possible want of accord between her and himself.
He responded cheerfully to her summons, which had

been conveyed by a note requesting him to call on her and receive in person her thanks for all his kindness.

"Is it quite certain," she asked, after a warm greeting of the self-constituted and persistent guardian of her rights, "that the Prince is going to be entirely out of debt?"

"Absolutely certain," said Vindex. "It is a great deliverance, and I congratulate you."

"I am sure," said the Princess, "we owe it very much to you, and you must not think me ungrateful, and self-willed, and opinionated, even if I have appeared so. Only where I could not see, I did not like to walk. Now I want you to add to all your good offices the final assurance, before we return to the dear old house, that every creditor is paid all that is owing him."

"Certainly," said Vindex, "that is so."

"Even Furax?" said the Princess.

"Furax be—" I grieve to record the fact that the good old jurisconsult had it, for a second, in his over-taxed temper, and on his too tempted tongue, to give utterance to a sentiment which would have been most unseemly and out of place. Fortunately, he checked himself in time, and the words he uttered reached the ears of the Princess in unexceptionable form.

"Furax be—ing no longer a creditor, has no concern with the settlement."

"But he was a creditor," said the Princess, "and the one who made the first trouble—and the only trouble—and who sold the furniture; and what I want to know is whether he will get his whole debt?"

"His whole debt, and claim, and proceedings, were bought in the beginning, and he was paid off. I bought them myself, for your benefit, and paid the money; I have been repaid, and we have no more to do with Furax, now, than with the man in the moon."

"I supposed you were at the bottom of the furniture sale. Prima found it out before I did. Of course, if I had known what you were doing, and that it was all for my benefit, I should not have behaved so foolishly. You must have thought very badly of me for going to the outcry, but I really could not help it."

"I think it was very natural," said Vindex.

"And very naughty, I suppose?"

"Your naughtiness does not interfere with me half as much as your goodness,—your overstrained and over-scrupulous honesty. My dear Princess, I am afraid you are color-blind in this matter of debtor and creditor. Why do you want to know anything more about Furax? He has been paid."

"But has he been paid in full?"

"He has been paid more than he deserved. He was only too glad when the failure took place to get half his debt, and so would all the creditors have been, could we have paid them at that time."

"Then the Prince still owes Furax the other half of his debt?"

"He does not owe him a single sesterium," said Vindex. "Pardon my saying it, but you are the most outrageously and provokingly honest woman I ever met. If everybody were like you, we could not get on a step. When a man is willing to take half his debt for the whole, he may sell it; just as you might sell the shawl you have on your shoulders for half its value, if you preferred having the money to keeping the shawl. When I bought the claim of Furax I became the owner, and whatever was owing him, before I bought it, became due to me."

"Dear me!" said the Princess. "Then we owe him, and you besides!"

"You don't owe him anything, and you don't owe me anything—we have both been paid in full."

"I cannot see how," persisted the Princess, "if neither Furax nor you ever got more than half the debt. Where is Furax?"

"He is dead," said Vindex.

"Then we must pay his widow."

"He was an old bachelor," said Vindex. "That accounts for his being so unfeeling. He had no wife, nor children, nor relations."

"I never heard of any one who had no relations, so long as he had any money," said the Princess; "but suppose he really had none, what then?"

"Then it would escheat and go to the State, and the politicians would probably contrive to get hold of it and squander it for base purposes."

"How dreadful" said the Princess. "I never knew before that escheating and cheating meant the same thing. There is no safety except in never owing a debt."

"That, madam," said Vindex, "is a sentiment which ought to be written, in letters of gold, on all the door posts and lintels of the land."

"What is to be done?" said the Princess. "I will never be satisfied till that debt is paid."

"We will do this," said Vindex, who had perhaps pushed the matter of the entire failure of next of kin of the deceased Furax, as he had the corruption of the politicians, somewhat beyond the possible reality; "we will make inquiry, and set apart a sufficient sum to provide for this balance of a debt which is due to nobody. What I want is to get you, and your husband, and children, back into the palace, which there was really never any occasion for your leaving, but 'all's well that ends well.'"

"We will go back on the Prince's birthday; it will come just a week from to-day," said the Little Lady, "and we will have Juventus and Prima with us, and you must certainly join us at dinner, won't you?"

The invitation was gladly accepted. The old jurisconsult, who had never been captured by the softer charms of the sex, was in love with the hard obstinacy of the Princess.

"I must reverse the usual method," he said to the Prince, "in dealing with your amiable wife. I censure her to her face, and praise her behind her back. She is the first woman I ever met who is entirely too good for this world."

"I have thought so for more than a score of years," said the Prince, "and have been only too glad and grateful that she is permitted to stay in it for my particular benefit."

"Look out never to fail again; she will want to pay everybody two hundred cents on the dollar."

"She knows no such word as fail," said the Prince, "and I trust I never shall, again."

# CHAPTER XXIV.

## HOME AGAIN.

THE restored family circle, gathered in anticipation of a birthday dinner, was a very happy one. The children were radiant with a new sense of delight. Juventus and Prima pleased themselves with the fancy that the renewed warmth and brightness of the palace were only beams from the same central source which irradiated the narrower precincts of their Via Sexta home. The Prince and Princess were contentedly serene.

"You and Juventus must break up where you are, and come to live with us," said the Prince to Prima.

"After a little," said Prima; "we cannot, just yet, bring our minds to the sacrifice involved in leaving the home we have made; and there is another source of embarrassment in deciding on the conflicting claims of half a dozen couples who, as soon as the rumor was about that you were to return here, have been besieging us for the refusal of our apartment. We have set a fashion that is going to be followed."

"Take your own time," said the Prince, "only remember that home, here, will hardly be home without you. But what has become of Vindex?

He is usually very prompt, and it is a quarter of an hour past the time."

Vindex came very late. Another quarter of an hour passed before he entered with warm greetings for all, but with something like a cloud resting on his brow.

" I am sorry to have kept you waiting, and more sorry for the cause of my delay. I bring bad news. Novus has come to great grief. He has broken to pieces. It has just come out that he has been engaged in the wildest speculations, which have gone frightfully wrong. He has used up all his own means and everybody's else he could lay his hands on, including what he had settled on Gloriosa, and has wound up by running away, probably beyond sea."

" I thought Gloriosa had her marriage portion secured," said Prima. " She told me so herself."

" Yes, but Novus contrived by orders in her name, which I fear were forged, to get control of the securities, and they are all pledged for his debts. Something may be saved, but it is a wretched business."

" It is very sad," said the Prince. " Novus had enough long ago, if he had only been willing to think so."

" To know when one has enough," said Vindex, " is to be wiser than the wisest. Novus took it into his head that he was predestined by the Fates to be a very rich man ; a ruinous illusion unless they predestine unlimited cash balances for every day's ventures."

"The craze after money seems to be taking this form," said the Prince. "Men are not satisfied with being rich, or trying to be rich; they must be very rich. I remember when the Chief Heralder published a little book, years ago, in which he gave a list of the wealthy men in the Imperial City, and every one who was supposed to possess a hundred thousand sestertia was set down in it. And I have known men retire from business on less than that in days long gone by. But the time of moderation is past. In the thirst for gain shallow draughts intoxicate, and drinking deep does not sober but drives mad."

"I almost wish for the time," said the Princess, "when very rich men will go out of fashion. They seem to do more harm than good; they do not produce half as much envy among people who have nothing, as they create dissatisfaction and a kind of overstrained imitation on the part of people who have neither the means to compete with them, nor the moral courage to forego the effort at competition."

"Your wish will hardly be gratified, at least in my time," said Vindex. The objects of worship which we create for ourselves, however unworthy, are the last to go to the moles and the bats, where they belong. The greed of gain and the idolatry of wealth are the two middle pillars on which the temple of Societas stands, and by which it is borne up, and there is no power mighty enough to bow down upon them and drag them to the earth. The tyranny of Societas has its main-stay in the compulsory extravagance and immoderation which it establishes as the rule of its service."

"What can be done?" said the Prince. "Everything goes to extremes with us. Magna Patria is a very young and fast growing nation, and, I suppose, must have its fling at everything before settling down to steady habits. If you ever tried to put a halter on a colt in a ten-acre lot, you know he would have his turn in every corner before you caught him."

"True enough," said Vindex; "and as the young people are very much in the ascendant in this young country, perhaps every fashion and folly must run its course; but, meanwhile, there ought to be some sound leaven in the great, seething mass; seven hundred, if not seven thousand, who are not bowing the knee to Societas when she requires the sacrifice of health, or good morals, or the rigid honesty which forbids transgression of the good old-fashioned rule of living within one's means."

"Or," said the Princess, "when she seeks to poison the very springs of the higher nature. Societas permits and even patronizes many things that are good and charitable, but we all know that the better life of which we are capable, and which so many honestly crave, cannot possibly thrive on her barren levels and in her unfriendly soil. She is of the earth, earthy, and so must they be who will be hers. But I believe the time will come when there will be people enough to create circles in which good sense

18

and gayety can go hand in hand, so that young girls
as gifted by nature in their heads as in their heels,
and yet who want to use both, will not find themselves clapped into a kind of debtor's jail by Societas because they will not pay her tax to the uttermost farthing."

"Poor, dear Gloriosa," said Prima, "that is where
she wanted to put me, on bread and water, because
I was obstinate enough to want my own little way
against Societas, and have my tiny bit of a fling in
the contrary direction from hers. I am almost
afraid I overdid my opposition and really offended
her, which I would not have done for the world.
She drove me to talking as I did, and if all I said
were written down or repeated, I fear people would
think I was pragmatical and a prig. But I am not
a prig. Am I, Juventus?"

"I never saw a prig," said Juventus, pausing over
his capon. "They don't grow wild in Dirigo and
I have not encountered them here. I really don't
know what a prig is."

"I know!" cried Secundus. "The Princess Pugnax keeps one. It is her grown-up grand-daughter.
She takes hold of things as if they were eels, like
this—."

And Secundus gave a vivid pantomimic illus-
tration drawn from his last summer's experience in
a fish-pond.

"And she talks the same way," exclaimed Tertia,
eager to impart her quota of information to Juventus, who, up to this time, she supposed, knew every-

thing. "She is perfectly horrid; she is going to establish a society to suppress toys, and story books, and dancing schools, and—"

"Children!" said the Princess, "You know it is against all rules to talk at the table about the peculiarities of people."

"Yes, mamma," said Tertia, subsiding into silence, but rather under protest. "Only we are not talking about people, but about prigs."

"I wonder," said Prima, "where Gloriosa is. She was still out of town day before yesterday. I would so like to help her—but what consolation can any one offer her? She is worse than widowed. And I love her so dearly!"

The Prince could not but recall his own hour of calamity; the loving help that had been to him like a fountain of living water in the desert; the sweet uses of adversity which he had known; the happy issue out of all his troubles which he had been granted, and which, while leaving him poorer in this world's goods, had enriched him with treasures he felt would never fail. He said, quietly, "May Gloriosa find shelter and succor from some loving heart and in some happy home."

They were still lingering at the table, late in the evening, detained not so much by its good cheer as by the entertaining talk of Vindex, who found in such companionship as this his best relaxation and recreation from the cares and toils which were his constant portion, when the Princess rose and excused herself, saying that she had been summoned to speak with some one who must see her instantly.

She entered the dimly-lighted reception-room. A woman waiting in the darkness suddenly threw back her veil, and caught her by both hands.

" Gloriosa ! is this you ? "

" Yes, it is I. I am distracted—almost beside myself. Have you heard that Novus has betrayed me, in every way, and is hiding, or has fled ? They are searching the house. It is dreadful ! I cannot stop there. None of my people are in town. I only came yesterday. I cannot go to any of my set. They are not friends for a trouble like this. I want you to help me. I heard you were home again, so I came here. It will kill me. To leave me penniless ! Oh the cowardice of it, and the shame of it ! I am only glad I have no children to be beggared along with me."

She sank on the chair the Princess had drawn toward her, while she still held her hand.

" My poor Gloriosa, I am so glad you came to us. There is a home for you here, if nowhere else. The Prince will advise you, and Vindex, the best, wisest, truest of friends, will take your case in hand. But just now what you need is rest and perfect quiet ; dismiss your attendant and stay with me. You shall see no one—not even Prima."

" It would kill me to see her now," said Gloriosa. " I have treated her badly ; but what a punishment to fall on me—and I gave him no cause. It was his extravagance—not mine—and to cheat

me out of what was my own. It is infamous!
Infamous!"

The Princess compelled her to remain. After
sending a brief message to Prima, to explain her
absence, and to save Gloriosa from intrusion, she
took her to the apartment adjoining her own; gently
forced her to take some needed stimulant; stayed
with her, soothing, calming and consoling her, as if
she were her own child; and, finally, when she was
quieted into a better condition, left her in the keeping of Patella, who was ready, at call, to wait and
watch beside her through the night.

"It seems wonderful," said the Little Lady to
Prima, when she bade her good-night, "that my first
duty, on re-entering this dear home, should be one
of service to this poor, sorrow-stricken soul; and
that Patella, with her humble ministrations, should
be able to bring to her, in her hour of anguish, an
unselfish succor such as all her lost wealth could
never buy."

# CHAPTER XXV.

## LAST WORDS.

MY story is told, and only a few words remain to be said.

Magna Patria, when last heard from, was enjoying a full measure of peace and prosperity. The novel idea is abroad in the realm that the great body of the good people who pay for carrying on their own government may, possibly, be better served by trained and skilled officials, than by raw hands, or by place-hunters and spoils-men, and that fitness for special duty is as safe a rule in the conduct of public affairs as in the domain of private industry. With this and other sound doctrines as the basis of social and political order, the Sisterhood need fear no adverse fortunes.

Novus never reappeared in the Imperial City. He led, for some time, a vagabond life, in distant foreign capitals, seen and shunned by his roving compatriots, and gradually fell into such obscurity that whether he were dead or alive few people knew, and still fewer cared to know. A small portion of Gloriosa's separate property was identified and rescued from the general wreck of his estate, providing her with a scanty income, and enabling her to flut-

278

ter, with clipped wings and faded plumage, in the gay parterres of Societas. The ancient friendship with Prima, revived in the shadows of her distress, became the best solace of her semi-widowed state.

Stella was traced, across the sea, to the home of her ancestors, whither she betook herself, with some of her kinsfolk, where she is said to have made a second marriage which, it is to be hoped, proved better than her first.

Patella was tenderly cared for in her declining years. The Princess, placing her in the front rank of the unselfish and devoted spirits of her sex, has never yet been able to put a limit to the multitude of the sins of Domesticus which are covered by the virtues of Patella.

Vindex made unavailing search for the last of the line of Furax, for whom the unclaimed sestertia were kept in safe deposit. As of old, the skilled advocate and wise counsellor, he came, at last, while unwilling to make any admissions, to be half ready to take it as proved, in the inner tribunal and shrine of conscience, that the truest sense of justice and the highest rule of honesty may sometimes be found, beyond and above the decrees of the Forum, or the mandates of the Law, in a woman's unreasoning instinct.

Juventus came rapidly to the front rank of his calling. He is satisfied with the repute and the substantial rewards he has gained, and with the assured certainty of leaving to his children and Prima's a name identified with the results of a career of hon-

orable toil. He foresees a growing conflict between
the interests of laboring men and their employers,
but he believes that the issue will finally be resolved,
not by the subversion of law, but by the establishment of a more enlightened reciprocity between
these mutually dependent interests; and while he
would have no man eat who will not work, he hopes
for the time when every willing worker shall have
his due portion meted out to him, according to the
rule of justice and the spirit of a true humanity.

Prima, long ago, became the centre of a radiant
circle whose bright philosophy of life takes no account of Societas and her shams. It asserts the paramount seriousness of work and the permissible gayety of play. It teaches that labor is the prime factor
of human happiness, as it is the first necessity of human existence and the sole source of permanent
wealth. It believes that contentment is better than
riches, and that there is nothing, earthly, nearer
heaven than home. On this broad basis, it can admit
to its companionship almost any one, except the
young men who fancy they cannot marry without
fortunes, and the young women who fear to wed
without doweries.

By this happy circle the Princess is held in high
esteem. She is an accepted oracle, with no ambi-
guity in her utterances. Her long and hard strug-
gles with adverse forces in the march and battle of
life have wrought out a wealth of experience from
whose ample stores she is ever ready to impart help
and encouragement to her struggling sisters. Hav-

ing solved the problem of Domesticus by her self-sustained supremacy on his own ground, she is striving to bring into the bewildering sphere of his activities, the elements of training and education which common sense and the universal judgment of mankind demand in all other departments of service. While her heart and her hands are fully occupied in maintaining many other good works, she knows of none whose use is more necessary, or whose results may be more beneficent.

The Prince is a confirmed optimist. The discipline of life has mellowed and refined his being. Some fruits, shaken from the tree, or plucked with rude hand, ripen better in the dark than in the sunshine and on the native stock. So it has been with his better nature, which, in his advancing years, is suffused with the glow of a true sympathy. He is in accord with the Princess in the constant faith that there is more happiness than misery in the world; more good than evil; more truth than falsehood; more honest men than rogues; that the human race, in spite of all its blunders and stumblings, is moving forward and not backward, and that in its bright future, under a better guidance than our own, there is hope for us all, including DOMESTICUS.

THE END.

# BRIEF LIST OF BOOKS OF FICTION

## PUBLISHED BY CHARLES SCRIBNER'S SONS

---

### George W. Cable.

| | | |
|---|---|---:|
| THE GRANDISSIMES. *New edition.* 12mo, . . | . | $1.25 |
| OLD CREOLE DAYS. *New edition.* 12mo, . . | . | 1.25 |
| The same in two parts. 16mo. Cloth, each, 75c.; paper, | | |
| each, . . . . . . . . | . | .30 |
| MADAME DELPHINE. 12mo, . . . . | . | .75 |

### Edward Eggleston.

| | |
|---|---:|
| ROXY. A Tale of Indiana Life. Illustrated. 12mo, | 1.50 |
| THE CIRCUIT RIDER. A Tale. Illustrated. 12mo, | 1.50 |
| THE HOOSIER SCHOOLMASTER. Illustrated. 12mo, | 1.25 |
| THE MYSTERY OF METROPOLISVILLE. Illustrated. | |
| 12mo, . . . . . . . . | 1.50 |
| THE END OF THE WORLD. A Love Story. Illustrated. | |
| 12mo, . . . . . . . . | 1.50 |
| *Complete Sets* (in box), . . . . . . | 7.25 |

### J. G. Holland.

| | |
|---|---:|
| SEVENOAKS. Small 12mo, . . . . . | 1.25 |
| THE BAY PATH. Small 12mo, . . . . | 1.25 |
| ARTHUR BONNICASTLE. Small 12mo, . . . | 1.25 |
| MISS GILBERT'S CAREER. Small 12mo, . . | 1.25 |
| NICHOLAS MINTURN. Small 12mo, . . . | 1.25 |

### Frances Hodgson Burnett.

| | |
|---|---:|
| THAT LASS O' LOWRIE'S. Illustrated. 12mo. Paper, | |
| 50c.; cloth, . . . . . . . . | 1.50 |
| HAWORTH'S. Illustrated. 12mo, . . . . | 1.50 |
| LOUISIANA. 12mo, . . . . . . . | 1.00 |
| SURLY TIM and Other Stories. Small 12mo, . . | 1.25 |

EARLIER STORIES.

| | |
|---|---:|
| LINDSAY'S LUCK. 16mo. Paper, . . . . | .30 |
| PRETTY POLLY PEMBERTON. 16mo. Paper, . . | .40 |
| KATHLEEN. 16mo. Paper, . . . . . | .40 |
| THEO. 16mo. Paper, . . . . . . | .30 |
| MISS CRESPIGNY. 16mo. Paper, . . . . | .30 |

## Frank R. Stockton.

RUDDER GRANGE. 12mo. Paper, 60 cents; cloth,     $1.25
THE LADY OR THE TIGER? and Other Stories. 12mo.
Paper, 50 cents; cloth, . . . . . .    1.00

## George P. Lathrop.

NEWPORT. 12mo. Paper, 50c.; cloth, . . .    1.25
AN ECHO OF PASSION. 12mo. Paper, 50c.; cloth,    1.00
IN THE DISTANCE. 12mo. Paper, 50c.; cloth, .    1.00

## Saxe Holm's Stories.

FIRST SERIES.

"Draxy Miller's Dowry," "The Elder's Wife," "Whose
Wife Was She?" "The One-Legged Dancers," "How
One Woman Kept Her Husband," "Esther Wynn's
Love Letters." 12mo, Paper, 50c.; cloth, . .    1.00

SECOND SERIES.

"A Four-Leaved Clover," "Farmer Bassett's Romance,"
"My Tourmaline," "Joe Hale's Red Stocking." "Su-
san Lawton's Escape." 12mo, Paper, 50c.; cloth, .    1.00

## H. H. Boyesen.

FALCONBERG. Illustrated. 12mo, . . . .    1.50
GUNNAR. A Tale of Norse Life. Square 12mo, .    1.25
TALES FROM TWO HEMISPHERES. Square 12mo, .    1.00
ILKA ON THE HILL TOP, and Other Stories. Square 12mo, 1.00
QUEEN TITANIA. Square 12mo, . . . .    1.00

## Edward Everett Hale.

PHILIP NOLAN'S FRIENDS. Illustrated. 12mo, .    1.75

## Augustus M. Swift.

CUPID, M.D. A Story. 16mo, . . . .    1.00

---

## The King's Men.

A Tale of To-morrow. By Robert Grant, John Boyle O'Reilly, J. S. of Dale, and John T. Wheelwright. 12mo, $1.25

## Virginia W. Johnson.

THE FAINALLS OF TIPTON. 12mo, . . . 1.25

## Mrs. E. Prentiss.

FRED, MARIA, AND ME. With illustrations. 12mo. *New edition,* . . . . . . . . . . 1.00

## J. S. of Dale.

GUERNDALE. An Old Story. 12mo. **Paper,** 50 cents; cloth, . . . . . . . . . 1.25

THE CRIME OF HENRY VANE. By the author of "Guerndale." 12mo, . . . . . . . 1.00

## Mary Adams.

AN HONORABLE SURRENDER. 16mo, . . . 1.00

## Count Leo Tolstoy.

THE COSSACKS. 12mo, . . . . . . 1.25

## Donald G. Mitchell.

DR. JOHNS. 12mo. *New edition,* . . . 1.25

## Julia Schayer.

TIGER LILY and Other Stories. 12mo, . . . 1.00

## Mary Mapes Dodge.

THEOPHILUS AND OTHERS. 12mo, . . . 1.50

## A. Perry.

THE SCHOOLMASTER'S TRIAL. 12mo, . . . 1.00

## H. C. Bunner and Brander Matthews.

IN PARTNERSHIP. Studies in Story-Telling. 12mo, 1.00

## Across the Chasm.

One vol. 12mo, . . . . . . . 1 00

# VALENTINO.

## By WILLIAM WALDORF ASTOR.

1 volume, 12mo, handsomely bound,  - - - - - -  **$2.00**

*"The style of the book is unaffected and musical. The descriptions are vivid and the dialogue is interesting. * * * Incidents are presented with dramatic art. The movement of the story never drags. The actors are natural and interesting, and the accessories are highly picturesque. The views of a strangely debased society, splendid in its luxuries and savage in its brutalities, a society which loved everything beautiful except virtue, and filled the palaces of the great with poets, painters, prisoners and bravos, are extremely effective."*—New York Tribune.

---

# STORIES by AMERICAN AUTHORS.

## "CABINET EDITION."

10 volumes, beautifully bound, gilt top. In a box.  - - -  **$7.50**

*This fine edition has been made necessary by the repeatedly expressed* **demand for** *this standard collection of American short stories in a form suitable for* **preservation** *on the library shelf or for gifts.*

---

# POPULAR DOLLAR NOVELS.

Each 1 volume, 12mo, extra cloth,  - - - - - - -  **$1.00**

| | |
|---|---|
| **THE LAST MEETING.** | **A WHEEL OF FIRE.** |
| By Brander Matthews. | By Arlo Bates. |
| **ROSES OF SHADOW.** | **WITHIN THE CAPES.** |
| By T. R. Sullivan. | By Howard Pyle. |
| **COLOR STUDIES.** | **ACROSS THE CHASM** |
| By T. A. Janvier (Ivory Black). | *A Story of North and South.* |

---

*For sale by all booksellers,* **or sent, post-paid,** *by the publishers.*

# CHARLES SCRIBNER'S SONS,

## 743 & 745 Broadway, New-York.

www.ingramcontent.com/pod-product-compliance
Lightning Source LLC
Chambersburg PA
CBHW021038030726
47496CB00006B/1598